PANTOMIME

PANTOMIME

Tina Bicât
with Ruth Staines and Colin Winslow

The Crowood Press

First published in 2004 by
The Crowood Press
Ramsbury, Marlborough
Wiltshire SN8 2HR

www.crowood.com

British Library Cataloguing-in-Publication Data
A catalogue record for this book is available from the British Library.

ISBN 1 86126 692 8

Photograph previous page: An 'elf' waits in the wings for his entrance
on the first night of the pantomime.

'He' and 'she' are used in an arbitrary manner throughout this book as, of course, both sexes
do all jobs in the theatre (except play a traditional Dame in a pantomime!).

All photographs are by the authors, unless otherwise stated.

Typeset by Textype, Cambridge

Printed and bound in Great Britain by Biddles Ltd, King's Lynn

CONTENTS

FOREWORD

Big-budget musicals today cost their producers millions to stage, and with luck they recoup the investment by running for several years. At the other end of the scale, producers look for straight plays with a cast of five or so, and a good economical two-hander is always welcome. So why is it that every year professionals and amateurs, grand theatres and village halls, choose to mount a spectacular show with a clutch of exotic sets, armloads of bizarre costumes, a bunch of special effects, and whose cast list may casually include a Giant, or Forty Thieves, or a plague of rats, or a gang of flying children, and which may rely for its effect on the convincing transformation of a pumpkin into a stagecoach? And to run it for only a few weeks, or even less? Are they mad? No! It's Pantomime!

Pantomime is unique in the affection it engenders on both sides of the footlights. For the professionals and amateurs on and behind the stage, there is the madness of preparation, rehearsal and performance, rewarded by the full-throated enthusiasm that roars back at them from the circle and stalls. For the audiences – many experiencing their first taste of live theatre – it is the warmest, silliest, most magical way to spend a couple of irresponsible hours. Or that's the way it ought to be. There's nothing worse than a pantomime that fails to enchant its audience. After all, it takes just as much hard work to put on a bad pantomime as a good one.

So be sure to put on a good one.

Tina Bicât tells you how. In this book she deals with the practicalities of rehearsals, props, costumes and effects. Like Tina, I have been involved in our small local provincial theatre's pantomimes over the years, but she has also worked in all manner of theatres, and knows the peculiar requirements and rewards of them all. Her sound practical advice in this book about the hard work, ingenuity and goodwill that are required will help anyone succeed in turning the madness of pantomime into magic.

Graeme Garden
February 2004

DEDICATION

For the pantomime companies and audiences of Chipping Norton Theatre.

ACKNOWLEDGEMENTS

Firstly, I would like to thank Ruth Staines and Colin Winslow for contributing to this book and for their expertise and experience, which I have drawn on throughout the book. I thank my brothers, Tony and Nick Bicât; Tony for the extract I have used from his pantomime *Robin of Wychwood* and Nick for the page of music from his song *Love Will Light our Way*.

Thanks, also, to: Alan Leith, Alison King, Amy Southeard, Anna Turk, Anne Byrne, Belinda Sharp, Beth Smith, Bob Sampson, Camilla Simson, Caroline Sharman, Charlotte Fenton, Charlotte Sabin, Chris Durham, Debbie Manuel, Dickie Metcalfe, Dudley Rogers, Elise Guest, Eloise Tarrant, Erin Wilson, Fiona Oram, Francesca Byrne, Gary Bates, Gwyneth Powell, Ian Nolan, Jack Pearson, India Shaw-Smith, Jay Johnstone, Jessie Caujolle, Jessie Chai, Jodie Tyack, John Gardyne, John Hester, Jonny Hoskins, Katie Burgess, Lee Brooks, Lisa Moule, Louis Greenbaum, Lucy Pearman, Matthew Herbert, Michael Lovatt, Millie Elmer-Menage, Nathan Chai, Oliver Naylor, Peter Pontzen, Peter Rycroft, Roy Cook, Rebecca Warrington, Robert Fenton, Robin Lannin, Rosie Archer, Sam Skillings, Sandra Everett, Simon Higlett, St Mary's College, Su Pittaway, Talia Lannin, Tamara Malcolm, Tanya Bailey, Tatiana Lannin, Tim Claydon and Tony Lander for sharing their experience of pantomime with me.

INTRODUCTION

Every Christmas companies all over Britain put the familiar characters on stage in different guises. Dick Whittington may be played by a sports star in one town, by an actor who has just finished playing Hamlet at the Royal National Theatre in another and by the local policeman's wife in a third. Theatres can be huge opera houses, college theatres or village halls. But the cast, professional or amateur, are all telling the same stories in a particular way and are part of a great tradition. The script, music, set and costumes must engage both adults and children; the actors must create fresh and true characters within the simple and familiar frame of stories we have known all our lives.

A front-cloth sets the scene for the audience before the performance starts.

Magic, romance, suspense and comedy are the lifeblood of most theatre performance, but there is one factor of our pantomime tradition that exists in no other theatre production. The audience has learnt its lines and been rehearsing its role every Christmas since early childhood. Every English-speaking person knows that 'Oh, no it's not!' should be answered with 'Oh, yes it is!' And that villains must be hissed and booed as they lay their evil plots.

A visit to the pantomime is a family outing. For many children it is their first visit to a theatre and to many adults it comes as a yearly treat; a reminder of an uncomplicated morality of right and wrong and of the fears and robust humour of childhood. It is not an elitist entertainment for a theatrically educated public. People don't come to be improved or enlightened or educated, though all those things may happen accidentally; they come because they know what to expect and they expect to have fun. The whole experience of coming to the warm theatre out of the cold Christmas street, of collecting the tickets and waiting for the lights to dim and the band to start playing, is coloured by the expectation in the adult audience of re-experiencing a particular traditional pleasure. Pantomime presents, without a hint of pomposity, the optimism of the happy-ever-after romance, bright colours, lovable tunes, glitter and laughter. And the unique and generous pleasure of enjoying a familiar joke with the hundreds of strangers in the audience!

The stories are familiar. *Cinderella*, *Little Red Riding Hood* and *The Sleeping Beauty* are stories that are told to children in many different languages. Even when the stories are not the same, the characters – the wicked stepmother, the poor boy who makes good, the enchanted

A visit to the pantomime is an exciting outing for the whole family.

prince – are universal. And the moral message, where the good triumph, the evil are vanquished and the poor inherit the earth, exists in every culture.

SOURCES AND CHANGES

The ancestors of our pantomime lived centuries ago. The basis, a simple story where familiar characters deliver a straightforward moral message, has been going strong for hundreds of years. Mystery and mummers' plays, harlequinades, burlesques, masques, melodrama, variety shows and music hall all hold traces of the pantomimes we see in our theatres today. The most recognizable ancestor, that rumbustious great-grandparent who brings us a Christmas stocking full of laughter, magic, romance, colour and surprise, is a Victorian. Despite the changes in style and content, he would recognize his descendants wise-cracking, singing and dancing on a modern stage.

There is a lot that the Victorian thespian would recognize backstage, too. Actors' stories and anecdotes in the green room, endless delays in rehearsals when the backstage workers try to solve the technical hitch in a magic

Pantomimes have always reflected contemporary interest.

The family enjoys their trip to the pantomime together.

effect, the nervous and silent tension in the wings before the curtain rises on the first performance and that unmistakable swell of sound, muted by the curtains and scenery, that filters backstage as the auditorium fills with excited children and their families – that sound which draws every member of the company together to share their pantomime with the audience.

British pantomime is a family affair. Each generation has adapted pantomime's guise to suit its time. As is the way of families, the parents mourn the loss of the old while the children forge the new. The pantomimes, in village halls or grand theatres, seen with the fresh eyes of childhood, are remembered by the adult through the transforming gauze of memory. And adults today, when so much entertainment flashes through the screens in

their living rooms, still want their children to experience the unique wonder of a trip to the pantomime.

EARLY MEMORIES

A child's first visit to the theatre is an inclusive experience. The queue for the tickets, the crowd of people sitting in rows, the ice cream in the interval, the tickets and the tip-up seats are remembered as part of the performance; the characters and magic, scenery and costumes they see onstage may stay in their memory forever. How often does a company present a production that has such an effect on its audience? Pantomime bears this serious

The ice cream queue in the interval.

responsibility lightly as it leads the young theatre-goer, roaring with laughter and engrossed in the story, to an intense new experience.

PRACTICAL MATTERS

Money

The yearly pantomime, despite its light-hearted nature, shows a much more serious side in the projected budgets of a year in the life of a theatre or company. Tickets are bought by people who go to the theatre at no other time. Three generations of a family come together. Not much, apart from a well-known Shakespeare play on the school syllabus, can rely on such an audience. The demand for seats means that booking starts early and the theatre coffers get an influx of money well in advance of the performance.

The huge increase in the number of people visiting the theatre has as an advantageous effect on its local profile and is an opportunity to attract more customers at other times of the year. The pantomime is the biggest money-spinner for almost every theatre: it subsidizes much of the budget for other less reliably popular productions throughout the year.

The sales of sweets and ice creams, the bar takings and any spin-off sales, such as 'magic' wands, pirate hats and badges, provide a further income boost, as does the programme if the size of the prospective audience warrants a large print run.

The pantomime can boost a theatre's yearly income and can subsidize less reliably popular productions.

Publicity

Creating a buzz of excitement in the community draws the public to the box office. The brochure, with its carefully chosen words, the flyers and any story or picture in the local papers start things humming and create an expectant excitement in the town shortly before booking opens. Well-known performers in the cast are a huge draw; there is a great fascination in the chance of seeing actors familiar from the screen in the flesh. Connections such as local schoolchildren in the cast are another. The reputation a pantomime has built up over past years is most valuable, as the outing becomes a part of the Christmas tradition of families who tend to return to the same theatre each year.

Established amateur companies are assured of good houses with their wide connections to local people. Reductions for group bookings, and publicity packs sent to primary schools can encourage group bookings in term-time when audience figures can feel the need for an extra boost.

The excitement is kept running throughout the booking period. Perhaps the best way is to feed a series of stories to the local press as Christmas draws nearer. The publicity material should be followed up with phone calls to encourage the press and to make sure that they arrive at the right place and the right time, and are met and welcomed. It is a waste of everyone's time to arrange photocalls and opportunities to meet the cast but then to

---

PHOTO OPPORTUNITY
Children's auditions for 'The Tale of Robin Hood'
22nd September at 4.30

The Directors of the Theatre's panto are looking for 6 young performers aged 8–11 and 6 aged 12–15 to star in this year's pantomime. Auditions will be held at the theatre on 22nd September. Auditions for 8–11 year olds will take place from 4.30pm; auditions for 12–15 year olds from 6pm. At 4.30 there will be a great photo opportunity to capture some of the region's most talented youngsters as they get put through their paces.

For further details contact the Theatre Marketing and Press Officer.

A press release of children's audition details to coincide with an advertisement in the local paper is sent out to create advance publicity.

make them inaccessible. Parking arrangements should be discussed if they might cause difficulty. Every effort should be made to make sure the press want to come and find it easy to get good photo opportunities and good stories – the rewards are too big to be left to chance.

Possible subjects to draw local interest:

* Hopeful children waiting to audition.
* Photos of some of the company with local sponsors.
* Actress who lives locally, or is known from television, talking about her role in the production.
* Set-building or painting in the theatre.
* Costume-fitting in theatre.
* Dame posing outside theatre in costume.
* Company in rehearsal.
* Members of the company visiting a local place of interest.

CONTINUITY

The pantomime audience in a town is built up year by year. The outing becomes as much a part of a family's Christmas as the turkey and the Christmas tree. The tendency of people to retain their family traditions, and the happy memories of their own excitement, encourages subsequent generations to want to replay the Christmas of their childhood and hand it on to their children. Theatres have a responsibility to the community they serve, and to themselves, to give these loyal and enthusiastic punters a splendid entertainment which will encourage the whole family to book tickets again next year.

Making up a billboard for publicity outside the theatre.

The box office is at its busiest during the pantomime booking period.

1 THE SCRIPT, ITS STORIES AND CHARACTERS

THE SCRIPT

Finding the Script

There are hundreds of pantomime scripts, most of which are based on familiar fairy and folk tales. The difficulty is in finding the right one from the huge variety available. There will be a fee to pay for using a script for public performance if it is still in copyright: if a due fee is not paid then the owner of the copyright has the right to insist the performance is withdrawn. This could happen at any time and no matter how much money and time has been spent. The law is subject to change and up-to-date information should be obtained (*see* the box on page 16).

Factors which may influence the choice of story:

* The list of pantomimes performed in the last few years. Choose a title not fresh in the memory – seven years is probably the minimum gap.
* The choice and publicity of other nearby theatres. Choose something different so that you are not working in competition; they may have different casts and styles, but the audience will choose by the title.
* The cast list. Can you afford Snow White's seven dwarfs (though it has been performed by one speaking dwarf and six cardboard cut-outs!).

Choosing the right script for the company and venue is vital.

* A well-known actor or actress in the cast – is there a possibility within the story for a suitable role for them?
* The need for a story that will allow a particular style of performance – traditional

Victorian, camp drag extravaganza, children's theatre performance, etc.

* Your instinctive feeling of what is right for the town and theatre audience?

Whatever you do and however you approach it, *Cinderella* hogs first place for the most popular story.

Points which help narrow down the field:

* The proposed style of the performance. It is no good starting off with a script written for performance by little children if you have a rip-roaring group from the local fire service to perform it.
* The number in the cast.
* The number of male and female members in the company.
* The necessity or otherwise of a chorus of dancers or singers, adults or children.
* The length and complication of production called for by the script. Is it possible to perform it in a few simple sets without the specialist equipment to fly characters or scenery? Or, alternatively, does it give you the opportunity to show off your theatre's impressive array of lifts, traps and revolves?
* Is the music included in the script? If not, can the company produce the money and/or skill to create it?
* How the script held your interest and imagination when you read it.
* Did you laugh when you read it?

The reasons for choosing a script are as varied as the directors, venues and budgets. The writers who create them are equally diverse in experience, interest and commitment to traditional or innovative perspectives on the genre. You must have faith in the script and believe its values are at one with the values of your company.

Permission to Perform

It is usually possible to get information about performing rights for both amateur and professional productions of pantomimes written in English from Samuel French of London, England (www.samuelfrench-london.co.uk), who have a huge list of pantomimes of which they can provide the scripts. Information can also be obtained from the script itself, which will give details on where to apply for permission to perform the work. No play or part of a play can be performed without this permission, though some establishments have a blanket agreement that allows them to perform within their schools or colleges.

Commissioning a Script

The disadvantage of commissioning a new script is that however much you have studied the previous work of the author, and discussed what you want, you don't know exactly what's coming until it plunks down on your office table. The advantage is that you hope to get exactly what you want, by an author whose work you admire, written especially for the company and theatre and for the style of production you have in mind. And you are in at the birth of a new creation.

THE CHARACTERS

The Dame

This extraordinary hybrid, this conglomerate child of ancient Greece and Georgian harlequinade, of sixteenth-century *commedia dell'arte* and Victorian burlesques, is a celebration of anarchic humour and has developed into the much-loved traditional character we see on the British pantomime stage. She is a man, and the audience know she's a man, though she is dressed as, and accepted as, a woman. They are with her in the joke in a way the other characters in the cast are not. She can talk to the audience, mock them, collude with them, sing with them, abuse them and flirt with them. Her vulgarity is rescued from censure by its delivery, which invites the audience to recognize the daring and delight of the naughty six-year-old shouting 'PANTS!' in school assembly, though her innuendo is often more adult ('Six months gone and no sign of Dick!') and her terrible puns produce groans from the audience.

She is allowed to hop in and out of the story in the most surreal manner. Reams could be written about her antecedents and influence, but any Dame worth her salt would soon debunk anything that smacked of the pompous or academic.

Traditional roles set her in place as a mature widow or spinster, past her prime but sexually alert, always on the lookout for a husband and usually getting one by the finale. Her opinion of herself is high and it is this self-confidence that enables her to ride, triumphant and ebullient, over the difficulties that would flatten any less robust character.

Despite the ambivalence of her role, and the risky nature of much of her humour, she is the children's friend. It is the Dame, in her bouts of audience participation, who knows their birthdays, welcomes their school or group to the theatre, talks to them and even, perhaps during the audience song, invites some of them onstage to participate in the action. The Dame, more than any other member of the pantomime company, must assess and control the audience and be able to improvise an immediate response to the varied, and often unexpected, repartee which comes from them.

The role is surrounded by tradition. Stock jokes, actions, phrases and business are repeated year after year, whatever the role; the only stricture of the tradition that is rigidly adhered to whatever the script, performance or company, is her dual role. She may be Mother Goose or Alderman Fitzwarren's housekeeper but she is also the Dame of all pantomimes and the link between the life of the world onstage and that of the audience in the auditorium.

The Principal Boy
Before the middle of the last century this was a role for an actress, and quite a glamorous role. Actresses used to specialize in the part and went on playing it when they were closer to middle-age than boy-age. In the last half of the twentieth century the role was adopted by men, often as a vehicle for a pop singer or other performer well known from television or the sports arena. His character is straightforward and painted in primary colours. The actor must perform the role with a particular core of truth that allows for an anti-naturalistic awareness of the audience when he asks for their help, and the utter realism that will win their wholehearted support.

In some productions a female Principal Boy, striding around in flattering breeches or fish-net tights still struts her stuff. As with the Dame, the audience knows she's a woman but accepts her as a man and, once again, they share in this joke which ensures their support. Male or female, adult or child, they must all want him to win. And she/he has the added advantage of being allowed to be knowingly sexy in a way that the Principal Girl is not. Beneath the singing and dancing, the strutting and audience participation must lie a true character and a genuine performance if the

The eyelashes, bosom, wig and hat: the transition from actor to Dame.

plot is at all important to the production. The Principal Boy and his Girl will carry the plot, and the audience, particularly the younger members of it, will get bored and restless if the plot is not clear and fast-moving. They need a strong clear line to follow that will hold up through the mayhem going on all round them.

The actress playing Principal Boy has to radiate a particular brand of sexual attraction. In other circumstances a young woman in fishnet tights and high-heeled boots strutting about the stage whacking a riding crop on her thigh and pretending to be in love with, and even kiss, another pretty young woman would produce a reaction in the audience that would hardly be suitable for the whole family, granny, toddler and all. But she struts and stands squarely. No pouting, bottom-waggling, bosom-thrusting or snogging; just the occasional gleam that tells those members of the audience who might be interested that she knows that they know that she knows . . . It is a powerful example of theatre's strength that it can, with a combination of narrative, laughter and pantomime tradition, bash an unsuitable reaction on the head with a foam rubber bopper, and do it without a trace of self-righteousness.

The Heroine

The heroine of the past had little to do except look lovely, sing prettily, engage the sympathy of the audience and get married. Women's lib has improved her lot in recent years and the modern heroine is often written as a young woman with a mind of her own though, of course, she still has to look lovely, sing prettily and live happily ever after. In her new personality she addresses the audience directly, often enlisting their help to jump the barriers to happiness that life puts between her and the hero. She is not a wishy-washy, goody-goody yes-woman. She is good, honest, and true and often, nowadays, sparky and intelligent as well, though she must still wear pretty clothes and find true love. The actress playing the role must retain sincerity despite the heightened and exaggerated displays of emotion demanded by the pantomime style. However up-to-date the audience and modern the heroine, she embodies a secret dream in the heart of all little girls in the audience, and probably in the hearts of some older girls as well.

The hero and his friends wait in the wings for their cue.

Pantomime has a duty to give romance to the audience and the heroine, whether she is Cinderella, Little Red Riding Hood or the Sleeping Beauty, must adjust her character to answer the aspirations of a modern audience. And still find true love.

Children Played by Adults

The Babes in the Wood, and others like them, are child characters who may be played by adults. The script usually gives these adult children a licence to misbehave and have adventures off the parental hook that puts the children in the audience firmly in their camp. Children display their emotions with instant physicality and adult actors playing these roles must reproduce, night-after-night, this energy, where every feeling is demonstrated with such frank immediacy. In addition they must avoid

any obvious imitation of child behaviour, as the difference between their age and that of the genuine children in the company would be thrown into high relief. The script can help by avoiding creating moments when the comparison is thrown under the spotlight.

The Comedy Double Act

The comedy duo – broker's men, scheming brothers or Chinese policemen – work as a team. It is rare to see one onstage without the other. It is a general, though not invariable, rule that one thinks he is clever and the other one is too stupid to know he's thick. In fact they are both silly. They, and their ridiculous behaviour, are a particular delight to the children who identify with the fact that this ludicrous pair are always in trouble with authority and unable to manage to get things

The comedy double act work as a team.

right, however hard they try. They often work as straight man and comic, and much of their comedy relies on perfect timing.

Whatever they do goes wrong. Their trousers fall down, eggs break on their heads, they trip over the smallest hump and, undaunted, they come back for more. All the tricks of slapstick and crosstalk are in their repertoire. Close teamwork and a familiarity with each other's style of work allows them to improvise together in their work with the audience and anticipate and work from each other's moves. Much of their comedy is physical and comes from gags where the audience feels itself one step ahead and anticipates the punch line or pratfall. Their skill in this case comes in building the gag, in holding the laughter back and in keeping the audience waiting until the joke breaks and the wave of laughter floods the audience. They are clowns with character and echo the foolishness in us all.

The Ugly Sisters are a particular double act of their own. They are not Dames, though they are men dressed as women. Neither are they drag queens. Together they present both a physical and a character contrast: perhaps one is tall, thin and rather arch while the other is short, fat and whiney. They display their nastiness quite openly to the audience with the naughty glee of evil children, and are proud to show off their spitefulness and greed. The frank and unapologetic delight they take in their beastliness is at the root of their comedy and allows us to laugh at actions that would not be out of place in a Jacobean tragedy.

The Good and the Bad
Tradition makes particular demands of these two faces of the moral coin. Pantomime goodies and baddies are either definitely good or thoroughly wicked. The good cannot be

Pantomime contrasts: one sister tall and thin, the other short and fat. Costume design by Colin Winslow.

dragged down to splash in the evil but it is sometimes possible for the power of goodness to reform the wicked ones – not, of course, until the end of the show. Traditionally the two can never touch: the good fairy appears from stage right in a pink light, the villain from stage left in a green one, and they never, ever cross or touch each other.

The good fairy, or her magic equivalent, often tempers her goodness with comedy. She may, while remaining good and magical, be scatty, a little bumbling, forgetful or comically inadequate in some endearing and human way which attracts the audience even more readily to her side. Indeed, she often asks for a little

21

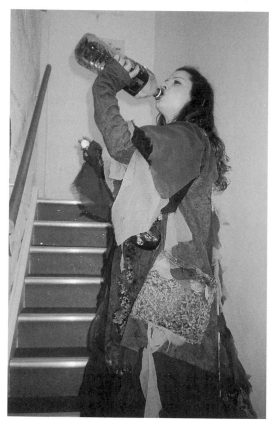

The witch takes her mask off backstage for refreshment.

help from them if her magic is wearing thin.

The villain, or perhaps villainess, on the other hand, delights in his or her own villainy. He loves gloating and boasting of his beastliness. His character is usually pompous and vain, and the attentions of the audience feed his vanity. He adores it when they boo and hiss at his dastardly words and their reaction incites him to lay bare his horrid schemes and openly rejoice in his beastly behaviour. He needs a weakness, preferably a rather silly and comic one with which the audience can identify: perhaps he is terrified of mice, or spiders, or the colour pink. The laughter provoked by

this weakness undercuts some of the real fear he may instil in the younger members of the audience, and will prevent him terrifying children so much that there are more children crying in the foyer than laughing in the auditorium.

His first entrance must show the audience that they are allowed to boo him, a reaction that has often been set up by a disclosure of his villainous nature by another character in a previous scene. The actor playing the baddy must control the reaction of the audience, encouraging it to add fuel to his characterization and suppressing it when the story demands to be heard.

Both these characters have a lot to contend with in the special effects department. Their entrances are heralded by showers of glitter, puffs of green smoke, lightning flashes and thunderclaps. They are the visible manifestation of the unshakable pantomime rule that good will always triumph over bad.

The Animals

The audience, and particularly the children in the audience, love the animals that appear in so many pantomimes. In the past, real and living elephants, camels, ostriches and other creatures have appeared on the pantomime stage. Today the most likely living contender for a smallish-scale production is the Shetland pony that pulls Cinderella's coach. Or the theatre cat making an unscheduled entrance while mousing! It is, however, a blessing on life backstage that most of these creatures are played by actors in costume. Anyone who has tried to entice a pony through the backstage areas of the theatre while Cinderella is doing her quick change into the ball dress, a set transformation scene is in progress and the entire cast are standing by in the wings ready to dance on for the ball scene, will undoubtedly agree. One's sympathies are with the animal: after all, they don't know the story or get to spend the pay, they can't go to the pub after the show and they probably don't realize how much pleasure they have given the audience. There are laws that govern the way performing animals must be looked after. Professional animals come with their handlers and it can be a safe option and a guarantee of their behaviour if their trainer can appear as perhaps a groom or coachman. It may mean an extra costume, but a costume that will pay dividends in the animal's behaviour.

In a non-professional situation, the animal will be a pet looked after by its owner and though the law relating to performing animals may not apply, common humanity and the pet's owner will, of course, take every care that the animal is not upset or maltreated in any way. In all cases a calm and competent carer will reduce the likelihood of a troubled or confused animal refusing to go onstage.

The other creatures in the casts – donkeys, ponies, cats, geese, cows and the occasional gorilla, camel or panda, should the script call for such exotica – are played by humans in animal costume. It is never a comfortable job. The best-made animal costumes or skins as they are called, are hot and airless, and restrict both vision and movement. In a two-man skin, where the front legs and head are worked by one actor and the back legs by another, the back legs can only see the actor in front and the floor beneath his feet. He has to trust in the front legs' steering power to lead him in the right direction and prevent him falling offstage or backing into the scenery. The front legs – head in the mask, which is often heavy and smelling strongly of glue – has to guide this cumbersome contraption by peering through gauze, through which he can see only a small portion of the stage. He probably has to manipulate the mechanism that flutters eyelashes or waggles ears at the same time. Those are the practicalities of the matter, and skins can be better or worse to wear. Actors, despite these inconvenient handicaps, manage to perform with great verve and develop marvellous characters in their roles as donkey or cow.

Other animals, such as Dick Whittington's

The pony waits patiently backstage for the moment when he will pull Cinderella's coach.

cat or Puss-in-Boots, have a character that is as close to human as animal, or is at least a mixture of the two. They will need to be sprightly and perhaps to talk, so their masks must enable them to be heard and to be able to see with ease. These human 'animals' work as much with the choreographer as with the director, as their movement is so essential to their role.

MAKING THE STORY INTO A PLAY

Most pantomime stories are fairy tales and they are usually short. The plots are simple and straightforward, and the final outcome is clear from the beginning. The bare bones of the tale must be clothed in detail that will enthral the audience for two hours and include the traditional set pieces that they expect. The plot of a pantomime is often very thin – to many, both artists and audience, it scarcely matters. They have come for the characters and the moments they have loved before and expect to love again. To others, the story matters very much indeed.

Whichever school of thought you support, everyone will agree that the characters must be strong and clear. Pantomime characters are simple people. They are good or bad, rich or poor, young or old, and it should not need complex analysis on the part of the audience to understand them and take part in their predicaments. However simple the plot, there must be a tension within it that makes the audience want the conclusion. The audience may be asked whether the hero should fight the giant but their decision, that of course he must, is created and forced by the story.

The first act is the time for establishing the characters; the time for custard pies to splat in the slosh scene and for the Dame's lengthy dialogues with the audience. By the second act the story has begun its headlong rush and the audience wants it to speed along to the happy conclusion, though the traditional place for the song sheet in the second to last scene of the show tends to make the wedding and the grand finale a visual, rather than an emotional treat. Pantomime tradition decrees that the last two lines of a pantomime are not

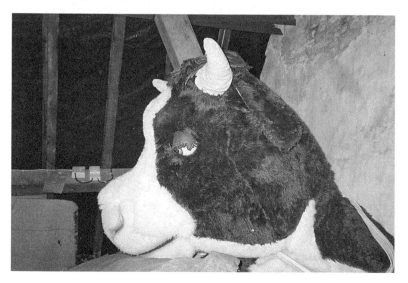

Daisy the cow waits patiently on the props table for her entrance.

spoken in rehearsal and are heard for the first time by both company and audience on the first night.

AUDIENCE PARTICIPATION

Many of the audience's lines are implicit in the script, though not actually written down. The question 'Which way did they go?' will create a furore of instructions and pointing fingers. A character creeping up on another will set off a chorus of 'He's behind you!' More subtle suggestions lead the reaction in a particular direction. The Dame sings:

'I was always a beauty it has to be said.
There was many a Beau keen to take me to
. . . wed!'

And invites the audience to call out a different rhyme to the couplet.

All through the pantomime there are places in the script where the audience will have a chance to play their part, and they will feel cheated and disappointed if the opportunity is not presented. A more reticent audience will need to be shown quite clearly that their participation is expected and invited. A rowdy audience will join in whether invited or not. The script, and the actors, must allow for both contingencies and everything in between.

Writing for a Family Audience

There can be a big difference in reaction between the audience at a matinee, which may be composed largely of young children, and the audience in the evening, when a more ribald humour may prevail. The script should allow for the appreciation of both groups. The great advantage of innuendo is that the deliv-

---

Death in Pantomime

There are deaths in some pantomimes and some pretty grisly ones – after all, it is not very nice to chop someone up and boil them in a jar of oil. The event is overlaid with glee or comedy that dilutes the horror. Kassim is chopped up into comedy foam boppers of arms and legs; Little Red Riding Hood gets munched up by the wolf but his dreadful burps and stomach rumblings make us laugh; the ogre is turned into a little mouse before he is gobbled up by Puss-in-Boots. Pantomime deaths are cartoon deaths and laugh aside the horror of nightmare.

The script is the starting point for director, designers and actors.

ery of the line can suggest a concept quite unsuitable for children in a way that can only be understood by those with a mind prepared to appreciate that particular brand of humour. Skilled actors will adjust their performance to suit the audience and will tread the delicate balance that allows both children and adults to enjoy the more risqué humour in a way that suits their understanding.

2   MUSIC

Music is the lifeblood of pantomime. It drives the action, leads the emotions and floods the audience with the high-spirited state that frees them to partici-

The piano is positioned so that the MD has a clear view of the stage.

pate in the unconditional pleasure of enjoying themselves. If you doubt the power of music, try listening to a dramatic moment on television with the sound off. This power is essential to a pantomime when laughter, fear, sorrow and romance succeed each other so rapidly through the story. There is no time for the audience to analyse such fast-changing emotions, and the music gives them an effortless short cut.

THE BAND

It is possible – anything is possible in the world of pantomime! – to perform with recorded music. But it is very difficult, and the skill required to make the recording and cue it with accuracy is rare, and expensively bought. Even when it is excellent in both these respects the performance is bound to suffer without the spontaneity and support of live musicians. A single piano player with a few percussion instruments can make an unbelievably good job of enhancing the performance.

They need to be versatile, these musicians of the pantomime band. And good at improvising. So much of the timing of the action onstage is led by the exchanges between actors and audience that no-one can be utterly certain how a performance will run. There can be an advantage to using a small band in their increased ability to improvise, and to improve or rescue the performer on any unexpected occasion during performance. An eight-piece band would be much more tied to the notes in their scores than a duo or trio working within glancing or whispering range of each other.

The Musical Director

The musical director (MD), as the name suggests, leads the playing of the music and rehearses the songs with the actors; he probably plays the piano for rehearsals and the keyboard in the band. He may have arranged traditional or specially written tunes for the voices and instruments in the production. He will probably book the band, though the composer or arranger will choose its make-up. The MD may be the composer, arranger and performer as well as the director of all the music and sound in a production. In a big-budget production he may lead a group of actors, chorus, band musicians, rehearsal musicians and performers in all the music of the show. The MD of a pantomime is as important to the rehearsal and running of the show as the conductor is to a grand opera.

The Band Line-up

The number of musicians in the band is usually dictated by the budget and the type of instruments by the composer or the MD. If there is only enough money in the pot for one instrument, it will probably be a keyboard. The choice between a straightforward piano or an electric keyboard, which can imitate the instruments of the orchestra and all sorts of sounds, depends on the style of the music, the player and the venue.

A larger band may be made up of keyboard and percussion, keyboard and a wind or brass player, or a multi-instrumentalist. The over-riding idea is to get the widest range of tone colours with the number of players you can afford.

Where to Put the Band

It is essential for the MD to have a clear view of what's going on onstage. In big theatres this

One band rehearses in the spacious rehearsal room, another in the theatre bar.

27

may be achieved with a closed-circuit television (CCTV) link-up. In theory this is fine and the band, in the case of amplified music, can be performing in a room well away from the stage. In practice the audience loses the chance to enjoy the visible signs of communication between the actors and the band. The best place for the band is in the orchestra pit between the stage and the audience or, if there is no pit, to the right or left in front of the stage. The MD will have a clear view of the stage and the band's participation in the show will be obvious and visible.

The single musicians who accompanied silent films in the past rose, bathed in their own spotlight, as if by magic through the floor

The percussion moves into the theatre.

Contact

The actors often refer to the MD by name during the performance: 'Thank you, Uncle Peter', 'Maestro, please!'; or the band is included in a gag. This audible, visible and affectionate contact cements the link between the three groups, actors, band and audience, and stresses how the band is an integral member of the performing company.

---

of the cinema. Their music replaced words, and entranced the audience and enriched the performance with a particular skill. When the only instrument is a piano, it makes sense that the audience should see both it and the pianist most clearly. Then, for some unfathomable reason, the possible shortcoming of a solo instrument will strike the audience as a particular and unusual advantage.

Lighting the Band for Audience and Efficiency
The band should be able to see their notes and music without drawing attention to themselves. A small downward light on each music stand should be sufficient, though, if there are lots of noise-making gadgets that have to be located in a hurry, a broader beam may be necessary. Where a follow-spot or a special (a light pre-focused on a particular point) is available, it can be used for highlighting the band when and if they are referred to on stage, or applauded at the curtain call.

SONGS AND TUNES

It is usual, when music is especially composed for a pantomime, to create the melody to fit the lyrics. The composer and lyricist work together to ensure that the scansion and mood of the work blend together in the best possible way. The lyricist will have an idea of the rhythm of the song, but the lyrics will probably need some adjustment to run with a tune in a way that feels musically natural.

Music Can Change the Meaning of Words

Simply stressing the phrase in different ways can change the meaning. And then there is the huge range of emotion and understanding of mood that can be evoked by the way the phrase is set. 'I *loved* you yesterday' tells a different tale from 'I loved *you* yesterday.' Or '*I* loved you yesterday.' And that's just the beginning!

Re-Using Existing Tunes

New lyrics, with a subject matter appropriate to the story, are often set to a folk song, nursery rhyme or pop song which is familiar to the audience. An addition much used in commercial pantomime is to echo what used to be a 'speciality act' in Victorian times by performing a contemporary pop-song that has only the most tenuous link to the story and action but which the audience connect to the actor. It is a strange anomaly that this occurs at two opposite ends of the pantomime scale. The amateur performer may have a song for which she is as renowned in her village as the chart-topping hit of the pop-star playing Cinderella is in the world of commercial music. They may both use the advantage of the audience's recognition of a familiar song linked to a familiar story. Audiences love to sing along: a well-known song, however inappropriate to the action, may result in them joining in, whether invited to or not.

Paying for Music

A fee may be payable if you want to use copyrighted recorded or sheet music for public performance. The publisher's name always appears on sheet and recorded music. Contact them and enquire. It is worth pleading poverty if you are short of money as there is no rule book, and fees can be negotiable. Contact the appropriate musicians' royalty collection society, the Performing Rights Society (PRS) in Great Britain, ASCAP or BNI in the USA, for current legal advice. Some establishments have a blanket licence that allows music to be used for performance and the fees to be allotted by the licensing body. It is the responsibility of the company producing the pantomime to make sure that music is paid for.

HELPING THE ACTION

Links

The music that underscores the pantomime does a complex job with a conjuror's ease. Imagine a scene of riotous excitement when a chase involves the actors scrambling round the auditorium, ad-libbing with the audience and creating a frenzy of excitement. This is followed by our hero and heroine singing a love song as they gaze into each other's eyes. The fast and furious music that helps build the tension of the chase changes in tempo and in key to the tender ballad. This musical change, perhaps accompanied by an alteration in the lighting state, can quieten and settle the audience and swing their mood from roaring bedlam to throat-tightening nostalgia with a speed and efficiency that no words could muster. Just as easily, with a sinister chord, it can splinter the mood again as the villain cackles on in his green spotlight.

Holding a Scene Together

The Dame sings the first verse of her song and then stops to unpack her ridiculous basket of props while talking directly to the audience. The 'till ready bars' continue underneath her words, hooking the song into the minds of the audience and adding zest to the lines until she finishes the basket business and resumes the song. The audience may not be aware of the music running beneath the words but they would notice the lack of it. This, and similar occasions, rely on the music to hold the baseline of a scene steady beneath the buoyant kafuffle in the limelight, and allow it to resume where the action was broken

Setting the Pace

Complicated business with props and audience participation can slow the pace of the action and it is often the job of the MD to re-establish the pace within a scene or cover an exit, perhaps with a variation of some bars of the character's song, while a scene change is established or another actor makes an entrance. After a bout of audience participa-tion, which often covers a scene change going on behind the front-cloth, the pace of the scene tends to drop. The band will play to cover the move and set the mood of the ensuing scene.dy Noises and Sound Effects

COMEDY NOISES AND SOUND EFFECTS

Live

Crashes and birdcalls, raspberries and wolf whistles are all in the day's work for the band. They may be called on to create the sound of breaking glass of an imaginary window, or to add an ache of enchantment to the moonlight with the fluting call of the owl. Some scenes, such as the slosh scene, when each dropped plate and splatted egg is reinforced by its clash or squelch, relies in part on the build-up from the band creating the tension and holding the full gust of laughter back until it is released by the throwing ('Shall I? . . . Shall I?') of the final custard pie. These extra 'instruments' of the band enrich the soundscape of what may be quite a small group of players.

Sound-editing software creates elaborate sound effects.

Recorded Sound

There are companies that produce CDs of sounds which can be transferred to a master CD or minidisk for use in production. Some of these can be bought in high-street music stores. There are also libraries that publish lists of effects and music under headings such as 'crowd, exterior laughter' or, 'atmospheres, seashore'. Contacts for these firms can be found in theatre trade papers and journals.

Sound-editing software is now widely available, and anyone with knowledge of computers will be able to create a CD of sound cues for their production. They will also be able to create the 'space' surrounding the effect; a frog croaking would not sound the same in the Grand Canyon as it would in the bathroom. It is more convenient, as well as helping to preserve the original CDs in excellent condition, to record ('burn') the sound cues for each production onto a single CD.

Music for Movement and Dance

The music, as much as the story, forms the inspiration for a choreographer. And not only for dance numbers. There may be movement sequences – the hero creeping up on the villain and freezing when he turns, or Jack climbing up the beanstalk and nearly tumbling – that are pointed and strengthened by the playing of the band. The director and choreographer decide what they want to happen and it is likely that the MD will create a piece of music that fits in with both the style and the action. It can be impractical, in a short rehearsal time, to contact an absent composer with an urgent request for another eight bars for Scene Five, particularly as these changes and additions are likely to occur at every rehearsal.

Creating Noises

The best sound effect is not always created by a recording of the real thing. The trick is to listen to the real sound and imagine how you could create a sound like it that you can control. For instance: cotton wool squeezed and rubbed between the hands sounds more like footsteps in the snow than the sound you might get after chilly efforts out in the fields; an axe slicing a cabbage sounds sinisterly like an execution; coconut shells are well known to sound like horses' hooves; and no-one will guess that the sound of Sinbad's conch shell is made by the stage manager blowing down the vacuum cleaner hose near a microphone. Experiment with the distance of the real sound from the microphone to get the most convincing sound. Closer means less interference, but it doesn't always sound best.

Some live sound effect hints:

* Breaking glass or crockery: put broken pieces in a lidded box and drop or rattle.
* Door opening and closing: a real lock or latch on a miniature door.
* Whip crack, gunshot or suchlike short, sharp sound: two lengths of thin wood with a dividing piece glued between at one end smacked sharply on a firm surface.

Rescue work – '. . . And the band played on . . .'

Every run of every pantomime has a disaster sometime during its run. The band is the rescue team when such disaster occurs. A good MD with a confident and intelligent sense of humour can redeem a situation that might otherwise result in a hiatus of, at best, ghastly silence and, at worst, fear and panic. When a quick change goes wrong and the hero is

Actors pre-record an offstage moment.

shouting his lines from the wings as the stage management desperately safety-pin his trousers together it is the band who, 'playing till ready' save the atmosphere in the auditorium from plummeting into embarrassed silence. In a more serious situation, when perhaps an accident onstage means the safety curtain must be lowered and the auditorium cleared, it is the music of the band that prevents a rise of panic in the punters.

Musical Jokes

Music can be very funny. Much comedy relies on timing, and music is a past master at getting it right. Musical jokes that are based on apparent mistakes work well when they create surprise, but they are likely to be misunderstood as embarrassing errors unless clearly pointed and very straightforward. The same goes for making people laugh with a pastiche of a familiar style or tune. The audience will be varied in age and experience, and a subtle musical reference may not be caught by everybody. The whole audience would recognize an operatic or football match song style, but they would not necessarily recognize a Verdi aria or a specific football chant.

The comedy double act, unconscious of each other's presence, back towards each other, bump, turn and scream. Would it be so funny if the anticipation of the audience was not heightened by the music echoing their footsteps and their moment of horrified realization, and accompanying their flight off the stage? Pantomime action is often pointed by music in the same way as are animated cartoon films; try watching one with the sound off, and then on, to understand how it works.

Incidental Music

The moment the band starts playing is the moment the show begins, though the sound of instruments tuning up has a fascination of its own that children never forget. The overture, usually a medley of the songs and dance tunes to come, heralds the lowering of the lights and the opening of the curtain: it would be a pretty bleak and unexciting start without it. More variations on the show songs forewarn and settle the audience in their seats for the beginning of Act Two and cover the scene changes. The walk-down of the pantomime, the final curtain call and the closing of the curtains are all accompanied by music, which holds the upbeat mood as the audience leaves the auditorium and sends them home smiling and singing.

The Song Sheet

This phrase refers to the words of a song, designed to be sung by the audience. They are written large and appear on stage from the wings or the flies to herald this well-loved scene. The traditional place for the song sheet is just before the walk-down at the end of the show. There are practical reasons for this:

* It doesn't take up much stage room and can be led by one character in front of a cloth, which hides the scene changes going on behind it and the cast and crew preparing for the walk-down and final curtain call.
* The audience is making so much noise themselves that they can't hear the noise of the hectic crew changing the scenery for the final scene.
* The actors are given time to change into their costumes for the finale.

It can, however, be a bad place from the point of view of the story, which by that point should be galloping helter-skelter towards its happy ending.

Not many people can resist the open-hearted affection and fun that bursts forth when we belt out a song with our families and a load of strangers. The words and the calligraphy must be easy to read: clear lower-case letters like the printed script in children's early reading books; no fancy gothic script or joined-up writing, and no words with spelling that might be tricky for young readers to interpret. The notes of the tune must fall well within the range of the poorest singer. Keeping the song somewhere between the A below middle C and the E an octave and a third above middle C is a good guide. And the tune must be easy to learn. The song is not a test of the audience's singing ability – though the traditional competition when the gallery and the stalls or the

The double act prepare to sing their number.

males and the females in the audience compete to see who can sing the loudest, pretends it is. It is the biggest chance the audience has during the show of joining in with the action onstage. The challenge is to overcome any self-consciousness in the audience and get them all enjoying the song without embarrassment or reserve. It's a mean and divisive gesture for an actor to pick on any member of the audience who is not joining in as there are always a few people who, for some reason or another, simply can't. For the rest it is a moment beloved by the audience, waited for and remembered.

MICROPHONES

The use of mikes on stage has a snowball effect. You may plan to use radio mikes for just the principal actors, but when the contrast between the un-miked actors and the boosted ones is heard in the auditorium, it becomes evident that general cover, at least, must be included to even things out. This snowball effect affects the budget dramatically and should be considered at an early stage of production planning.

Radio Mikes

Audiences have become used to seeing actors with strange contraptions round their faces and seem able to ignore them, although they can look like warts or surgical devices to the uninformed. The best place to hide a personal microphone that picks up the sound of the actor's voice is at the centre forehead where, with luck, it will be hidden by the hair. It can be attached to the skin with toupée tape, or some other sticky tape. The wire can run over the head under the hair or hat, down the back and to the power pack on the belt. The sound operator is responsible for activating and deactivating the mikes according to cue, and for checking and replacing batteries. Where there is no sound operator and actors are responsible for switching the power on and off at their entrances and exits, it is wise to instil a habit that the stage management checks this has been done. Mikes can't choose: they will relay the actor cursing in the dressing room or gossiping in the wings, or some other sound not suitable to the pantomime plot, as readily as they will a ballad. Where there is a sound operator in the company he will be responsible for collecting all mikes after the show and recharging them. Otherwise this important task becomes another vital point on the stage manager's list.

Other Types of Microphone

Float or flown mikes provide a general cover for relaying the sound from the stage and are usually used in conjunction with radio mikes. Rifle mikes can be focused to pick up the sound within a narrow range. Offstage mikes can be used to boost live sound effects or enhance the voice of an actor making vocal sound effects offstage. A reverb or effects processor can be used in conjunction with an offstage mike to create doomy echoes and ogres out for blood in vast halls.

TEACHING SONGS

The company is likely to be made up of actors who can read music and actors who can't. Nonetheless, it is a great help to everyone, when learning songs, to have the music as well as the words. It will also help, when rehearsal time is very limited, if actors are sent a tape of the songs before the start of rehearsal. People who could not read the tune and sing it straight off find the score a great help when trying to remember what they have heard. At least they can tell if the notes go up or down and the slightest experience will teach a novice the time values of the different notes. The best situation is to have the words of the song written out below the notes in the relevant place, so that both can be read at the same time.

Though it's a generalization, the usual rule is that the top line or the line that holds the melody is the easiest to sing, the bottom line is the second easiest and the harmonies sandwiched between the two the hardest. It is as well to remember this when teaching company choruses: choose the weakest singers for the

Words written beneath the relevant notes in the score. Copyright Nick Bicât.

easiest parts. The order of work most likely to succeed with a group of singers of variable experience is:

1. Play and sing the whole thing while the learners follow their scripts.
2. Sing through the song phrase-by-phrase with the singers repeating after each section.
3. All limp through the whole song, singing and playing the tune along with the actors.
4. Rework the phrases of any difficult bits.
5. Sing the whole lot through.
6. Sing the whole thing with the accompaniment as in performance.
7. Ask the actors to bring to your attention any places where they are unsure.

It is helpful to actors if they record the songs on a personal tape so that they can learn and practise the songs alone alongside their line-learning.

Helping Actor/Singers through Difficulties
The cast is likely to contain a proportion of actors who sing, as opposed to trained singers. There are times when an actor will find a song, or part of a song, extremely difficult. If things are still going badly after individual work on the song, the MD has to make a choice. Perhaps the song should be altered to make it easier to sing, or transposed to a lower or higher key. The MD may have to steel his musical ear to a less pedantic mode and ride mistakes that the actor may not have the time or skill to rectify. The most vital outcome of any decision is that the actor should retain confidence in his or her ability to put over the number to the audience. All songs, sad or happy, slow or fast, need to be performed in a

The MD works with an actress on her solo.

confident manner that assumes the interest and sympathetic understanding of the audience. A song performed by a doubting Thomas will sink like a stone. And it's very hard for an actor to assume this confident approach if he doubts his ability to do a good job.

Teaching Children

The rules outlined above apply when teaching professional children who are used to the work. But often 'The Children of the Village' or 'Gnomes' in the cast list are schoolchildren from the local youth theatre or dance school, and are not trained singers. It can be a bit of a battle to get them to produce a good sound. All children can make a loud noise: you only have to listen to the

sound of a playground at break time to hear the splendid, energetic quality of sound they produce with no apparent effort. They can even do it when running, jumping and scrapping, which is more than can be said of many adult actors.

But line them up in front of the piano in the rehearsal room and their energy dwindles to a well-behaved polite little voice that must be coaxed to grow to fill the auditorium. Most companies cannot afford personal microphones for all the children, so it is essential that they make a big enough sound to be heard above band and adults. The volume is not so problematic when the company numbers are performed to the accompaniment of a pre-recorded version of the song.

One trick to open out the sound and leave a polite junior-choir sound in the classroom is to get them to sing a song they know really well such as *Happy Birthday to You*. Putting in a comic and slightly naughty word in place of the name will help to loosen things up – not many children can remain on their guard when singing 'Happy birthday dear snot-face'! Smiling while singing helps to open up a good sound and is a method that will be understood, whereas more technical advice on voice production might jam the lines of communication. Avoid asking children to sing a line they are unsure of alone – it's better to make the whole group sing it several times and the child who is having trouble can sort out the problem by imitating the others.

Children who come from the same group might be encouraged to learn the songs in advance with their teacher or youth theatre leader. This will give more time in rehearsal to develop the sound you want, and their familiarity with the words and tune will free their concentration when learning the actions or dance routine that accompany the song.

3 BEFORE REHEARSALS BEGIN

The director, having accepted the job and read the script, will begin the pre-production discussions with the various members of the company. That the play is a pantomime gives a direct lead to the style of production, particularly as each venue or company will have developed its own particular tradition over the years. A director will have been approached who is sympathetic to their particular style. The first meeting is likely to be with the production manager.

PRE-PRODUCTION DISCUSSION

Company Structure and Money

This meeting, which may become a series of meetings, sounds as if it is all about money and a lot of it is; but the artistic framework of the show will be discussed with equal attention. The controller of the budget may be the theatre manager or director, the production manager, perhaps the treasurer of the committee in an amateur company, or have some other title. Whoever it is and however informal the company, there must be someone who has an overview of the total budget for the production. She will arrange terms of employment, negotiate with agents and artists and, at an early meeting, will present the proposed breakdown of the budget into the separate sums to be allotted to each department. It becomes the responsibility of the heads of different departments to manage their respective sums of money and account for them. The production manager will arrange for the repayment of money spent, and the paying of salaries, expenses and bills. She will provide each department with a float of cash which will be accounted for by keeping receipts of any money spent on the production. Companies may have accounts or arrangements with certain suppliers and details and order forms for such transactions will be available. Sometimes a supplier may offer goods or services in exchange for a credit in the programmes and that can prove a financial advantage to both parties involved.

The proposed budget will be discussed with the director as it affects both the casting and the presentation of the work. There are many questions to be considered. Perhaps those most to the fore are:

* Paying for the venue, the script, the music and the company.
* Advertising the show.
* The number of actors to be employed and the scale of their salaries.
* The length of the rehearsal period.
* The number of designers to be employed

Expenditure

This is a list for a medium-sized venue. Of course every pantomime company will have different expenses, some more, some less.

Writer's fee inclusive
Composer's fee inclusive
Set designer's fee
Set designer's expenses
Lighting designer's fee inclusive
Choreographer's fee inclusive
Chaperone
Laundry
Actors' basic
Actors' holiday pay
Actors' overtime
SM enhancement
DSM basic
DSM holiday pay
ASM basic
ASM holiday pay
Stage management overtime
Musician fee
Actors & stage management travel
National Insurance
Musical director's fee
Actors' subsistence
Stage management subsistence
Children
Auditions
Set
Costumes including design
Costume maker
LX & sound
Transport
Props
Get out
Sundry
Management travel
Sweets
Contingency

(set, lighting, costume, sound).
* Whether to employ a full-time choreographer.
* Whether to employ a full-time musical director.
* The necessity or otherwise of a full-time rehearsal pianist.
* The venue for rehearsals.
* The size of the band.
* The set, its complication and construction and painting, or hiring costs.
* The costumes, their complication, the number of changes and their construction or hiring costs.
* The show's running costs, including pantomime specials such as explosions, glitter and custard pies twice nightly, piano tuning and the huge amount of laundry and cleaning engendered by actors belting around the stage under hot lights for four to six hours a day.
* The salaries of chaperones to look after the children of the company.

It is always wise to allow a sum for unforeseen contingencies both in the general budgets and the budgets allotted to the separate departments. It is impossible to foresee the exact progress of the production period.

All this, or most of it, may take place without the director having any input until much later on in the proceedings. He or she may be employed simply to turn up on the first day of rehearsal and sort things out from there. If the show is being directed by someone in the cast, an assistant director may be called on to run the technical and dress rehearsals while the director is performing and so cannot see, from the audience's point of view, what is happening on stage.

Early Meetings with the Production Team
The production team will have been assembled for an early meeting with the director. They will

The theatre office is a hub of the production, whether it is one room that doubles as dressing room and wardrobe or a formal, well-equipped workspace.

have been chosen by a combination of the director and the production manager, who will have taken into account that they will all have to work together and that their styles and temperaments must not clash. It will be helpful if, before this meeting, everyone has read the script, even if it is an early draft and subject to change, or at least knows the story and where and when it is supposed to take place.

The director will talk about his thoughts on the production and try to convey the style he envisages. He will facilitate an exchange of ideas between the different departments and try to assess and expose any areas of disagreement, misunderstanding or budgetary dangers. It is most helpful to have the cool and rather impartial ear of the production manager and stage manager to steer a reasonable path when ideas become wild and impractical. Most of the people at this meeting will have been employed because they are good at having ideas and making imaginative leaps. They do not always have the same regard to money, time and finance as the more down-to-earth

members of the company.

Talk and questions about the general style of production will lead on to more particular matters which vary according to the demands of the script. Here are some examples of avenues that demonstrate the wide scope of matters, both practical and artistic, which may be explored:

* Can the witch double with the cat to save the cost of another cast member?
* Will the costume designer design and make the cow skin, or will it be farmed out to a freelance skin maker?
* Can the trap under the stage accommodate two actors at the same time or is there only room for one?
* How much space will the upstage right entrance need to allow the gypsy caravan to come onstage?
* When must the designs be completed in order to allow time for scenic construction, painting and costume making?
* Does the set designer envisage a particular

Key members of the company meet for discussion at a production meeting.

range of colour and if so what do the costume designer and lighting designer think about it?
* Will the choreographer have the music before rehearsals start in order to create the routines before the start of rehearsal?
* Will the actors' voices be amplified?
* Will the management allow one seat to be unsold throughout the run in order that a member of the cast can be planted there for a particular gag?

This might sound, and very occasionally might be, a huge meeting with a formal agenda in a board room. It probably won't be. However solemnly it starts, people are too interested and too full of ideas for a formal discussion. The size of the meeting may vary from two or three people round a kitchen table to a room full of experienced practitioners. But the boiling of ideas won't be any cooler.

Composer and/or Musical Director

The composer will have read the script and the lyrics, and the first discussion with the director will relate to the style of the music. A decision will be made about whether the music should have a contemporary or a period feeling, whether it should have a reference to a particular genre, how big a band can be allowed for by the budget, how big a chorus and the number and sex of the cast. The type of song – ballad duet or company rock number – will be mooted. At the next meeting the director will hope to hear the songs, or at least some of them, in rough form and the number of band players, the instruments they will play and their position in the performance will be settled. A decision may need to be made on whether the set designer needs to create a particular space for an onstage or visible band and whether the band members will be in costume. Before casting begins the vocal range of the actors must be established and the necessity or otherwise of casting actors who can play particular instruments.

Choreographer

The director will work through the script with the choreographer, marking the places where a group of villagers dance on the green in one scene, the principal boy and girl waltz alone in another and woodland creatures dance in the forest in a third. The choreographer must know the numbers of people who will be on the stage, the level of their ability and whether he will be working with children or adults. Will there be a troupe of trained dancers who do nothing else, or will the actors be doing all the dancing? In the latter case he may create something that may be closer to choreographed movement than dance. Effects and characterizations that rely on physical movement, such as flying, giants, fights or animals need expert help from the choreographer or movement specialist. First and foremost must come the music, no matter how rough the form, as he cannot start work without it.

Set Designer

After an exchange of ideas relating to the general style of the show, the director and set designer will work through the script, detailing the changes of scene and any particular ideas or effects that may not have become apparent from the reading of the script. They will determine which scenes will need to take place in front of a front-cloth while a compli-

cated scene change takes place behind it, and the position and number of entrances and exits.

Lighting Designer

The discussion with the lighting designer will be quite general as much of the more detailed work that the director and lighting designer will do together will occur at the light-plotting session once the set has been erected. Ideas which affect the budget such as follow-spots (lights that are moved to create a spotlight which follows on particular actor) or ultra-violet-lit scenes may cost extra as the theatre may not have the equipment in the building. The same is true of sound and other special effects such as snow and smoke.

Costume Designer

The discussion with the costume designer, once the period and style has been agreed on, will tend to concern the complication of quick changes and doubling rather than the aesthetics of the work. Rough drawings may help make sure the ideas in the designer's mind

The designer uses a ground plan of the stage to discuss the position of exits and entrances with the director.

41

The follow-spot and its operator – an expensive addition to a small budget.

coincide with those in the director's. More detailed drawings will be discussed at a later meeting – it is much less expensive to make changes at the drawing stage than after the costumes have been made or hired.

Stage Management Team

The presence of the stage manager at any of these discussions means that the practical element is much more likely to be taken into consideration. It is all very well imagining the marvellous moment when the phantom coach and horses career across the stage, but the stage manager will know that the space in the wings is limited and that a major set change is going on at the same time. This may affect the entrance through which the carriage can appear, which in turn may affect both the width of the entrance (set design), the position of the lights (lighting designer) and the way the coach is made (carpenter). The stage manager is the most likely person to pinpoint potential problems and so prevent a waste of time and resources.

Amateur Production Meetings

The amateur group may perhaps work to a pattern that is familiar to the group – the key members of the company remain in place year after year and this naturally speeds up the pre-production discussions as people already have an idea of their place in the scheme of work. New members are added year by year to the society and are absorbed into their roles with the support of the more experienced members. In effect, an amateur company has more in common with a traditional repertory company where a company of actors and technicians work together on many different productions and are well acquainted with each other's strengths and weaknesses. The same decisions have to be considered, but the group experience of past years will be helpful both in pointing out and solving problems.

Cutting the Script

There will be a strict timing for the show. Many of the audience will be young, and a two-hour show including the interval is a good length to aim at. The children will be able to hold their concentration on the story and enjoy the bursts of audience activity that punctuate it. With two, or even three, shows a day actors have to have rest time, and time to eat and the stage management have to have time to change the set as well. The front of house has to be cleaned, and ice cream, sweet and programme stocks replenished. The director has to keep a clear eye on how long the show is running. It is a great waste of everyone's time and money if a scene has to be cut at the dress rehearsal to allow for the changeover between performances.

Cutting the script may be more than a simple matter of timing. The first factor to consider is the story. Anything that detracts from the clarity of the narrative line should be looked at carefully. The points where the plot is held in abeyance, perhaps for the audience song or a company dance, will need a firm line for the actors to regain the attention of the audience as the plot resumes.

CASTING

It is often said that the success of any production lies in the way it is cast. Actors in pantomime need to be versatile, quick-witted and physically strong. They will be working to a very demanding schedule both in rehearsal and in the number of performances.

Rough designs that give a starting point for discussion between director and costume designer.

Cutting the script to fit the tight schedule of three shows a day in the pantomime season.

Professional pantomimes are usually performed twice, sometimes three times, daily and there is rarely a moment during the show when an actor has time for a quiet rest in the dressing room. The short time they have offstage will be used up with changes and perhaps offstage singing. The only day off in the whole run may be Christmas day, and the difficulty of bank holiday travel means that they may not get home for that. Amateur companies have a less demanding schedule and a shorter run, but they have to rehearse and perform whilst working at their everyday jobs and running their homes.

Arranging Auditions

The pantomime season sees more actors in work than any other time of the year. Many actors work at other jobs during the rest of the year and perform on stage at no other time. Professional and amateur companies begin the casting process by creating a breakdown of the character list. Professional companies will send their cast breakdown to agents and amateur directors will inform the members of their

society of the roles available.

Members of amateur companies are often well known to their director, who may have a mental idea of who will play the characters at an earlier stage of pre-production than will his professional equivalent. Most amateur actors come from a familiar and local pool while professional actors are spread out all over the country. The audition process of amateur companies varies with the size of the society but has the same objectives as any casting process – to assemble the best company they can to do the job.

Professional Auditions

A character breakdown list is sent out to agents who will put forward those of their clients who they think might be suitable for the roles. Actors known to the company may be suggested and an availability check will be made to see if they would be free to take the job.

The production manager and director will receive CVs detailing training, experience and special skills (such as trumpet playing, stage-

Cast Breakdown

MEN

MR WARRINGTON:	Fifty-plus. Father to Beauty and her sisters. Genial, urbane businessman who has fallen on hard times. Baritone.
MISS McWHITTERER:	Dame. Forty plus. Scottish accent throughout.
DIDSBURY:	Twenties. Young, enthusiastic gardener at the Beast's castle. Lots of 'Hello Kids' business. Works as a double-act with
MAURICE:	Thirty plus. Butler at the castle. Tall, cadaverous, pessimistic. Tap dance an advantage.
BEAST/PRINCE:	Twenties. Doubles fearsome beast and charming prince. Good-looking, clean-cut. High baritone. Must be an excellent singer.

WOMEN

BEAUTY:	Late teens/early twenties. Beautiful of course! Feisty and spirited heroine. Strong soprano voice and excellent dance skills essential.
EUPHORIA:	Twenties/thirties. Beauty's sister. Tall and thin. Works as a double-act with
ASPHYXIA:	Twenties/thirties. Euphoria's twin sister. Short and plump.

Example of a cast breakdown for Beauty and the Beast *by John Gardyne*

fight training or tap dancing), their singing range and a photograph of each actor. From these they will make a shortlist of those they would like to audition; they then contact the agents with the dates of rehearsal and performance, the role for which they are being seen and the time and place of the audition. Actors will bring a prepared song, and may be asked to bring a prepared speech though it is more usual for them to be asked to read an appropriate section of the script. A rehearsal pianist will play the accompaniments to leave the MD free to assess and remember each performance.

The director, musical director, choreographer and possibly the production manager, writer and composer may be present at the audition so it can be a pretty daunting occasion for a young professional. Inexperienced actors will have to be outstanding in some respect to succeed in a pantomime audition, as their lack of experience and of track record in coping physically and vocally with the demands of a long run makes them a considerable risk for the company. Famous names or those well known to the company and the director may be offered the work without audition.

It is impossible to understand what an extraordinary job acting is if you haven't been present at an audition. And how brave and determined actors are. They wait around together outside knowing the people they are with are their competitors and then are called one by one into a large bare room. There is an upright piano at one end and a large expanse of bare boards at the other. Several people are

45

Directors select what they hope will be the perfect cast at an audition.

sitting behind a table full of papers and photographs talking quietly, earnestly and privately. It's really very bleak and about as far from the happy-go-lucky atmosphere of the pantomime performance as you could get. In this atmosphere, after a few words of chat and introduction, they will be asked to read some lines from the script and, having handed their sheet music to the accompanist, perform their song. And in those few minutes their ability and personality and their likelihood of performing the role will be judged.

It is well worth giving them every help and encouragement to show what they can do. A polite and friendly attitude is a good start. Actors are sometimes asked to read the same speech in a different way or a different accent, to improvise response to pretend audience comment, to work on a small scene with the director or another actor, or to dance. If the style of music in the production differs greatly from the actor's chosen song, another may be asked for, or a request made to put over the original song in a different way. They may be asked for an upbeat number if a downbeat one has been sung, or the reverse, and perhaps a scale or two to ascertain their singing range.

The actors may have a rough time of it, but so do those who are casting. They are looking for someone who sounds and looks right for the part and can sing and move well if the role demands it. The nature of pantomime means they will also be looking for actors with a particularly strong ability to engage with the audience and improvise round the unexpected occasion. The composer or musical director will be looking for a voice with an appropriate range and the ability to put over a number.

For those watching the auditions and choosing the actors, it is a feat of concentration and memory helped by an instinct for judging an actor's ability. They need to remember and take notes on each possibility because, though the first auditionee at ten o'clock in the morning may have seemed perfect for the role, the twenty-fifth contender, much later in the day, may perhaps prove to be even better. So somehow they have to remember the performances of all those different people. It is essential for the success of the pantomime that they assemble a company that will perform well together. The first audition may result in a further shortlist, particularly when, as in a double act, actors must work as a duo. Pairs of actors may be called to work together before the final decisions are made and the roles are offered to the actors.

Children's Auditions

A company using local schoolchildren in its pantomime may hold an open audition. The publicity this creates is irresistible, but for those auditioning it can be heartbreaking or infuriating depending on their temperaments, and always frustrating. There are always a great many children who want to be on stage. There will always be many more girls than boys. It is usually possible to tell in thirty seconds if the child has any chance of getting the part. Hard-hearted practicality would divide them into the biggest groups that could be accommodated in the space, having first sent away any child who was too tall. Then to ask them all to walk across the stage and run back and send any no-hopers, which will probably be about 80 per cent of the children, home without more ado. Not many directors would be so careless of the children's feelings.

The less hard-hearted might work through the exhausting day like this.

1. All the children should be asked to bring packed lunch and a drink if the day is likely to be a long one, and clothes which are easy to move in.
2. Each child should give their name, age, height and contact details to be noted on a list. In exchange they will be given a large, clearly written stick-on name to wear.
3. The person in charge should note on the list whether they are a boy or a girl – Alex, Nicky, Sam, and others, could be either.
4. The children should be divided into groups of twenty to twenty-five and taught a simple routine – something like three steps to one side, three to another, a jump and a turn.
5. They should all be asked to repeat this together and encouraged in every way to feel relaxed, happy and as if the whole thing is fun rather than a test. Music will help.
6. Those watching will write down the names of those who will proceed to the next round.
7. A break, possibly for lunch while lists are revised and the children who are unsuc-

cessful are informed in the kindest way possible that they are no longer needed. This should be done in a way that precludes any dialogue with the parents and is bound to be painful to the unlucky children, parents and those who have to make the decisions.

The remaining children, divided into groups of three or four, will be asked to sing something well known together and perhaps to have a short chat with the director. *Happy Birthday* is a good bet to start with as everyone knows it. The first four lines of *Somewhere over the Rainbow* are also revealing as they are easy to learn and start with a jump of an octave which, without the feeling of an exam creeping in, will tell you if the child can sing. The successful children, plus reserves, can be informed on the day or by post or phone afterwards.

The exact demands of rehearsal, performance times, commitments and all other details should be made absolutely clear in writing to parents and guardians before finalizing arrangements.

Any direct contact with parents once the whittling-down process has been started should be avoided; some parents find it very hard to cope with the fact that their child has not been chosen and it is horrible for parent, child and chooser to have to explain why.

The pantomime is cast, the scripts prepared, the music composed and the designs drawn. Costumes and set are under construction. Contracts are signed. The piano is tuned. The stage management has prepared the rehearsal room. Posters are all over the town advertising the pantomime. And the cast arrives in the town ready for the first day of rehearsal.

Rehearsals: Monday 3 November – Wednesday 19 November
Performances: Thursday 20 November – Saturday 10 January

COMMITMENT REQUIRED
There will be two teams of 5 children. If chosen each child will appear in approximately 40 performances. Each team will do an equal number of performances, with one doing the opening night, the other the closing night. There will also be two 'Swings' who will cover approximately 10 performances and any other occasions when the children in the two original teams are unable to perform e.g. due to illness.

A rota will be drawn up to indicate who is on duty at any given performance. At this stage we cannot specify the particular dates that each child will be performing on, therefore total commitment over the above period of time is required. Unfortunately it is not possible to swap performances (except in extreme circumstances such as illness).

Performances run 6 days a week including Saturdays and some Sundays, Christmas Eve, Boxing Day, New Year's Eve and New Year's Day. There is no performance on Christmas Day.

TRANSPORT
All transport to and from the theatre is arranged by parents/guardians. As there are two performances a day this can involve a lot of dropping off and picking up.

SCHOOL
Due to matinée performances during term-time, each child will be absent from school for approximately 5 full days and 2 half days. It is the responsibility of parents/guardians to obtain written permission from the child's school for them to participate. The Theatre will then make an application to the County Council regarding a performance licence for each child. More information about this will follow.

DURING PERFORMANCES
The Theatre employs an approved chaperone during the pantomime who will be with the children at all times. Children will be on stage at various points throughout the performance but will be given breaks. The performance will last approximately 2 hours (including interval) with the earliest performances starting at 10.30am and latest evening performances ending at 9.45pm. See attached schedule for further details.

REHEARSALS
Rehearsals commence on Monday 3 November. For the first week each child will be required to rehearse every day from 4.00–6.00pm at the theatre and probably for a period on Saturday. The following week the schedule is likely to be similar. The rehearsal period becomes more intense in the week of Monday 17 November, when the Company move onto the stage for technical and dress rehearsals, a period known as the Production Week, with the first public performance taking place on Thursday 20 November at 2.00pm. Although a schedule for the week will be drawn up nearer the time, it is realistic to assume that it will not be possible for children to attend school for much of that week. Precise timings and further details of the Production Week will be confirmed nearer the date.

Example of information given to the parents of the children chosen to be in the pantomime.

4 THE PANTOMIME IN REHEARSAL

irecting a pantomime is not quite like directing any other show. It is like rolling a farce, a children's play, a musical and a variety show into a well-constructed ball that is strong enough to cope with being chucked vigorously, and apparently carelessly, backwards and forwards from the stage to the audience without breaking up into fragments or dropping to the ground. Not an easy task. Particularly when there are so many technical matters, both for performers and backstage crew, which need confident and well-rehearsed timing and precision.

Some pantomimes are scripted, rehearsed and performed as rigorously as any other musical show. Others are worked on in a way that is closer to a variety show or a review, where everybody performs their set pieces – the Dame's song, the slosh scene, the company song and dance in the painted village square – and the various turns are stitched together with a story based on a well-known tale. It can happen that a well-known member of the cast, perhaps playing the Dame, will not be there for the early rehearsals, but will slot a ready-made performance into the show at a later stage, in much the same way that a great tenor will slot his habitual performance of a particular role into a grand opera: some travel with a full set of costumes as well as their performance. Most theatres and companies, amateur and professional, produce something between the two.

EARLY WORK

As the director reads the script for the first time he will begin to develop a concept of the way the show will be. The characters and their relations with each other will become clear, and a feeling for the look and rhythm of the show will solidify. Pantomime demands particular attention to the overall pattern of the show and the progress of the story. Despite the many jokes, songs, dances and bouts of audience participation, the storyline must come through clearly or the attention of the audience will be lost. It is traditional, but not invariable, that the prologue is followed by a company number (the village green, the market place), has an exciting set piece or a cliff-hanger before the first interval (will our hero survive?) and ends with the wedding and the walk-down. The rhythm of the piece ebbs and flows between these points and the director gives the audience periods of quiet, calm attention (the princess sings of her hopes and fears for the future), fear and fury (the appearance of the villain as he tells the audience of his evil intent), riotous comedy (the Chinese cooks create a meal) and breathtaking magic

49

(the beanstalk grows). It calls for a sure and well-prepared mind to keep the journey of the performance chugging steadily on despite all these obstacles.

Cutting the Script

A pantomime may have to be cut to fit into a particular time slot. Some are performed three times a day and actors must have time to rest and eat. The technical crew must have time to eat and to reset stage and props, and the front-of-house staff need time to clean the theatre and restock the bar and ice cream sales points. It can be difficult to judge the final length of a pantomime as the audience participation in the action is an unknown quantity (and Dames have been known to improvise at length!). Judge carefully the possible addition to the length of the show and cut the script accordingly. Quick changes of set or costume must be considered in case they are dangerously affected by the cuts. Make sure the cuts do not make the story difficult to understand.

Dance

The pantomime choreographer will have read the script, heard the music and will have discussed with the director the sort of mood and style of dance they both envisage for each scene. This is likely to be a rough suggestion: a morris dance/folk dance feel in the company number in the market place, a sultry tango for the Dame and the baddy. He may have been at the auditions and have assessed the dance skills of the cast. Or he may arrive on the first day of rehearsal knowing how many people he will choreograph but with little idea of the skill and experience of the performers. He will have worked with the music, and may have set and noted complete dance sequences. Or he may arrive at rehearsal armed with a knowledge of the music and the script and some rough ideas that he will fine-tune when he can assess the ability of the performers.

Children in the company may come from a local dance school and will be used to learning complicated routines. On the other hand, a child who is dancing for the first time, and whose rehearsal time in the theatre must be fitted round school attendance, needs simple routines that can be learnt quickly. The audience love to see children dancing and will enjoy the unprofessional performance of the inexperienced child every bit as much as they love the impressive routines of the little professionals.

TIME

Paying for Time

The amateur pantomime director has a particular advantage over the professional – they will have more time. This is a question of money. Amateur pantomimes sometimes employ a professional director, but the pressure of paying the actors and technicians is removed. Pantomime companies are big. There is no way anything approaching a traditional one can be performed with a cast of three and one stage manager. The stories demand more actors, the genre calls for singers and dancers, sets and costumes. The rehearsals need a pianist and a fairly spacious rehearsal room. A choreographer and musical director can hardly be dispensed with. All these people cost money and the longer they are employed for, the more money they cost. Consequently, economy demands that rehearsal periods in professional companies are kept as short as possible.

Amateur companies do, though, have to work with the disadvantage of there being times when people are not able to come to rehearsal due to the pressure of work or study. After all, their work in the theatre is part of their social calendar as well as a serious interest. The director of an amateur or student company may insist, when casting, on the necessity of the company being present at all rehearsals where they are needed, but there is no way they can enforce the rule. Their only recourse is to re-cast, and that is not always possible as the first night looms nearer. Most amateur companies are keen and committed and problems of this nature occur only rarely. It is, however, important to make clear when casting just how much time and commitment will be needed – then at least everyone knows what to expect.

Time for Experiment

The director short of rehearsal time cannot afford to spend days on experiment and improvisation; indeed, some of the cast, particularly if they are experienced pantomime performers, will tend to get very edgy if they feel they are not getting to grips with the shape of the performance fairly quickly. Actors have songs and dances to learn as well as their lines and moves, and costume fittings of complicated designs can eat into the working day. This can create problems in the company as directors used to working in more experimental or less technically complicated productions may be used to beginning the day's work with exercises and games. Few actors object to a quick vocal and physical warm-up session with the company, but lengthier workshop improvisations and character games may well alienate members of the cast who have experienced the speed with which the technical skills must be mastered and perfected in such a short time.

The Schedule

A schedule detailing the work to be accomplished in rehearsals can be created before the company first meets for the read-through. It will end up being only a rough guide, as it is impossible to predict exactly how much will be accomplished each day. But it will give a framework on which to base the daily schedule and will remind everyone of the different stages that lead to the opening night. It will also ensure that enough time is given to music and dance rehearsals, which may take place away from the main rehearsal room.

Making Best Use of Space and Time

With so many things to rehearse in a short time, the best possible use must be made of the available spaces. The director may suggest an initial schedule well in advance of rehearsals, but it is inevitable that this will change. Some scenes will prove simpler to stage than others, some actors will find certain sections harder than others, the writer may wish to rewrite, and the comic scenes will need to be worked out. In one day an actor may block a scene with the director, have a session with the musical director on a solo number, and then join the whole cast to rehearse the dance finale with the choreographer. The stage manager must dovetail all these requirements and keep the whole production team informed as to what is going on where, so that possible problems that arise during rehearsals can be ironed out before the technical rehearsal. At the end of each day the stage manager will, in consultation with the director, produce a schedule for the following day to let each actor know when and where he will be required. She will also circulate a list of the wardrobe and stage management notes that have cropped up during the day's work.

Communication between departments is vital when rehearsals and technical work take place in different venues.

Communication

Communication is vital and can be achieved via a central notice board for rehearsal schedules, costume fittings, and so on. Stage management should reinforce this by checking that all departments have the information they require as the production progresses.

The director and stage manager will work out a daily schedule of each day's work to post on the company notice-board. The rehearsal working day is extremely demanding and everyone will work at home in the evening to prepare for rehearsal next day. The actors must know which lines, songs and dances to prepare, the stage management need to know which scenes must be set and which props must be in place in the rehearsal room. The choreographer and MD want to know when actors will not be needed in the rehearsal room and so can be called to music or dance rehearsals. The wardrobe can attempt to arrange fittings so that actors are not losing rehearsal time. The whole company must know what they will be doing, if they are to be ready for each day's work and rehearsals are to be smooth and productive.

THE FIRST DAY OF REHEARSAL

The company assemble on the first day of rehearsal. Most members of amateur companies will know each other, or will at least live in the same area as the rest of the company. Some people in a professional company will have worked together in other shows or have met at auditions or production meetings. Others will be resident staff at the venue. Most will be meeting for the first time. This collection of people will be working closely together, some far enough from their own homes to spend Christmas and New Year together. They will certainly all get nervous, tired, excited and (with luck) triumphant together, and see each other at their best and their worst. Like it or not, they must all bond into a company, and a friendly and well-organized first day of rehearsal can inspire an auspicious start.

The Green Room

The green room is the company common room. Posh or tatty, large or small, it is the company's place of comfort. There, the cast and crew chat, laugh, grumble, do their cross-

Date	Time	What?	Led by	Location	Who?
Mon. 8th	10.00	Movement	Choreographer	Rehearsal room	Baron
	10.00	Voice	Musical Director	Bar	Marion
	10.00	Act I sc. i	Director	Stage	Dame, Robin, Sam, Janet.
	10.00	Costume fitting	Designer/maker	Wardrobe	Tom
	11.30	Act I sc. ii	Director	Stage	Tom & Harry
	11.30	Movement	Choreographer	Rehearsal room	Marion & Robin
	11.30	Voice	Musical Director	Bar	Sam & Janet
	11.30	Costume	Designer/Maker	Wardrobe	Dame
	13.00	LUNCH	*****	*****	*****
	14.00	Movement, Act I sc. ii	Choreographer	Rehearsal room	Children
	15.00	Act I sc. iii	Director, MD	Stage	Company
	15.00–16.00	Act I sc. iii	Director, MD, Choreographer	Stage	Company including children

Example of a daily schedule.

words, go through their lines and drink coffee and tea. Two actors rehearse their fight in one corner, using their fingers as the prop swords they will use in rehearsal; another couple go through their lines, the costume-maker discusses the position and size of a pocket with the Dame; the DSM and ASM check through a prop list and everyone tells anyone who will listen the theatrical anecdotes that chatter through every green room. This room, and perhaps the theatre pub, will be at the heart of the company's social life for the length of the pantomime season.

First Read-Through

The read-through takes place on the first working day of rehearsal, and the whole company meet together. The script will be read and any cuts or additions given out. It will be help-ful if a model of the set is on show and the different set changes displayed as the reading progresses. The songs will be played and sung, perhaps in rough form but in the correct place in the script, and any effects that are planned will be brought to the attention of the company during the reading. The actors will be able to see designs of the costumes they will be wearing. The idea is to give everyone a rough idea of the look and sound of the whole show.

Rehearsals after this reading will tend to be fragmented, with actors rehearsing the script, songs and dances in different rehearsal rooms, while the technicians are at work in their separate departments. Gradually, as songs and dances are learnt and rehearsed, they will be incorporated into the general rehearsals. The whole company – actors, technicians, directors, designers and crew – may

Different aspects of the show are presented to the company at the read-through. Here, the designer demonstrates scene changes on the set model . . .

. . . an actor studies his costume design . . .

. . . and the composer plays through the songs.

not all meet together again before the dress rehearsal.

Company Policy

The production manager should inform the company at this first meeting of various items of company policy and business. Arrangements for the payment of salaries, allowance of complimentary tickets, the theatre smoking policy and any other business that involves life in the theatre. A tour of the building should be arranged so that actors know where to find the various offices and departments of the theatre.

Company Health

It is the responsibility of everyone to try to keep as fit as possible during what will be an arduous period. Colds and sore throats, let alone the dreaded flu, can sweep through a company and only the biggest commercial companies have understudies on call. The company may arrange, through the theatre doctor, to make flu jabs available to the company free of charge – it will be company money well spent. Most actors and dancers prefer to do their own specific warm-up exercises to prevent strains and injuries, though sometimes an actor will lead a company warm-up session and the MD a voice warm-up.

Some theatres arrange a reduced rate for the company at the local gym or swimming pool. Contact numbers should be available for a local doctor and dentist.

THE WORKING DAY

What's Different about Pantomime?

The big difference between directing a pantomime and directing any other sort of show is the familiarity of many of the cast with the style and even the content of the script. Many actors have played the same sort of role – the old father, one half of a double act, the principal boy and of course the Dame – before. This is a double-edged sword. It has an advantage in that their experience speeds up rehearsal time and the actor is prepared for an audience response. It has its disadvantages when the director looks for a fresh or different approach to the part and meets resistance or uncertainty in the actor. Of course, this is rare because most actors, particularly experienced ones, are used to taking all sorts of direction.

The other most particular difference between rehearsal for pantomime and that for any other show is that an all-important member of the company is not present at any of the rehearsals. It is the audience, whose lines and reactions cannot be pre-rehearsed. Anyone in the rehearsal room during rehearsal could offer to participate with boos, hisses, heckles and 'he's behind you!' to accustom the actors to a reply and to help with the timing of the show. The children of the company may be particularly useful in this regard, and it will help to engage their interest during the longueurs of rehearsal.

There will be some audience members who try to give awkward responses or preclude the

An early rehearsal takes place, with the script in hand.

The Slosh Scene – Controlled Mayhem!

The logistics of rehearsing this scene are perhaps the most demanding of the pantomime's preparation and call for the closest communication between director, MD, choreographer, stage management, wardrobe and actors. The timing has to be precise, the noises from the band bang on cue, the costumes practical, the props exact and the floor surface reliably un-slippery when wet – and the presentation of all these technicalities must appear effortless to the audience. The actors have to combine complicated business with custard pies, water and flour with most precisely timed movements. They may be singing and dancing and juggling kitchen equipment at the same time, and will certainly be moving fast. Working alongside this physical concentration there must be an acute awareness of the audience reaction, of how to hold back a laugh until there can be a hiatus in the action long enough for the audience to let rip.

It is not the mess that gets the laugh. It is the anticipation and the reaction. The actor who receives the pie in the face has four distinct moments:

1. The moment the audience realize what's coming and he, apparently, doesn't.
2. The moment of the splat.
3. The moment of the audience seeing him covered with gunk and his realization of the fact.
4. The wiping off of the gunk.

action, either on purpose or with the delightful and extreme innocence of childhood that led a little six-year-old to rush onto the stage to rescue the heroine. It is as well to warn young actors of this pantomime hazard, though nothing but a ready wit and experience can provide a solution.

Blocking

The director, who may not in other cases formally 'block' (work out the moves for each scene in advance), will probably do so in the case of a pantomime as there are so many technical considerations that have to be worked alongside the actors on the stage. Directors have all sorts of different methods of laying their plans, but most are based on the principle of moving something (counters, pebbles, sugar lumps) that represents the actors around the ground plan of each scene. Time is likely to be so short that actors will be able to work more

quickly if they are presented with moves that they can then write in their scripts and learn with their lines. Actors who are working to a very tight schedule, particularly when dancing and physical comedy or fights are involved, prefer to have definite guidance from their director. These moves, of course, are subject to change and discussion. But agreement, or even disagreement and reworking, can be achieved much more quickly if there is something concrete on which to base the discussion.

Pantomime blocking tends to involve a lot of getting people on and off the stage, and making sure that the cast are in the right place for the many exits, entrances and quick changes of set and costume. The space in the wings must always be considered. Imagine a troupe of dancers waiting to come onstage and perform a front-cloth scene while a complicated scene change happens round them backstage, or the Dame and a group of children are doing a quick change in a blackout, and you can see why careful blocking provides a way of averting delay and re-blocking at the technical rehearsal.

Fights and Falls

There is a lot of fighting in pantomime, both comic and cliff-edge, and a lot of falling about. All these moves are choreographed and rehearsed so that they can be performed with absolute precision, particularly if weapons are involved. There is no room for improvisation; even a blunt wooden sword can do serious damage. Falls may look funny to the audience: the funniest falls, however, can be the most difficult to perform and to time, and are practised over and over again.

Dancing and Choreography

The blocking that goes on in the rehearsal room is vital information for the choreographer, particularly when, as so often happens, he is working in a different rehearsal space. He must know when and where actors and dancers come onstage and where they go off, or if they are already onstage playing a scene when the sequence begins. This information makes it easy to slot the pre-rehearsed dance sequences into the scenes at a later stage of rehearsal. The standard within the company can vary between trained dancers who can learn routines quickly and perform them with ease, and actors who have little dance experience. There will probably be a troupe of children whose ability, unless they all come from the same local dance school, will vary as much as the adults'. The settings created by the choreographer will depend on the dance experience of the company and the time

Actors rehearse complicated moves again and again to ensure that they are safe and look easy on stage.

available for rehearsal. The dances are created and rehearsed by the choreographer, and it prevents confusion and saves time at later stages of rehearsal if the director gives clear information as to what is happening onstage during each scene.

Onstage Furniture

There is rarely much onstage furniture. Scenes take place either in front of a front-cloth, when the narrow strip of stage limits their movement, or on a relatively empty stage. The sofas, tables, standard lamps and chairs that belong in a naturalistic set are out of place in pantomime. When they are present they can exist out of context; a pantomime standard lamp doesn't have to appear to be plugged in to an electricity supply. Everybody will accept without question that it can light up when necessary by some power peculiar to the pantomime stage. The front door through which the Alderman Fitzwarren appears may be painted on the backcloth, but he can appear from the wings when he enters the scene. Jack may climb up the beanstalk with great effort to reach the giant's castle in the sky, but others will stroll into this lofty palace as if it were on solid earth. Pantomime sense is bizarre, but apparently impossible events will be accepted without question by the audience. The logical progression of the story needs to hold a firm baseline to support the outrageous happenings onstage.

Rehearsing the Children

Pantomimes have children in the cast. For most of the rehearsal period the children will come to the theatre for rehearsals after school. The actors may have been rehearsing a scene in which they appear during the day, and the children will be slotted into the scene during the last couple of hours of the day's work. The advantage of working this way round is that the adult actors already know what will be happening in the scene and will be able to help the children to land up in the right place and catch the right atmosphere for the scene. If there has been time for the children to work alone on the scene beforehand, it will make the rehearsal run more smoothly.

The cast warm up onstage before a dance rehearsal.

IN THE REHEARSAL ROOM

Characterization

Pantomime characters are not complex. Actors in naturalistic plays unravel every nuance of the script, and spend hours in researching the background to a play in order to understand the complicated inner life of the characters they play. They dig and fish out the motivation behind the words and deeds performed onstage. This work may seem wasted on a pantomime script. The characters are straightforward. Heroes are good, villains are bad, old people are very old and cats can talk. Ask not the reason why, though if you do ask and delve a bit, you are likely to become fascinated by the psychological whirlpool that seethes beneath the clear fairy-tale sky. The actor and director trying to get a show on in a fortnight must shut Oedipus, Freud and their complicated friends in the cupboard till later, and concentrate on producing genuine, clear characterizations of the people in the story they are telling that will allow the audience, whatever their age, to recognize the sort of person they are portraying.

Fragmented Rehearsals

In the initial stage of rehearsal, when the blocking is taking place, the director, MD and the choreographer may be working on the different scenes; actors not needed in the main rehearsal room will be working with the MD or the choreographer elsewhere. In companies where the director is also the choreographer and directing the music himself, it will be of great benefit to his concentration if he has a rehearsal pianist or, at least, someone working a tape or CD player so that he can concentrate on the artistic rather than the technical content of the work.

The Stage Manager 'On the Book'

The right-hand man and the chief help and comforter of the director in rehearsals is the member of stage management who is taking notes of every move, the lighting, sound and effects cue for the prompt copy, and keeping a list of anything that will need to be relayed to the different departments after the day's rehearsal is over. It is extremely difficult for a

Hero and heroine rehearse their love scene in prosaic rehearsal clothes and surroundings.

director to concentrate on rehearsing the piece while simultaneously keeping notes of what is going on. Therefore even in the smallest companies, where stage-management help is very short, the note-taker – known as the member of stage management 'on the book' – cannot be dispensed with. To do so is to lay up trouble for the work ahead, and ensure disaster and bedlam at the technical rehearsal.

Learning the Script and Moves

It is essential that the actors learn their lines as early as possible, because of the physical movement, the timing and dancing and the number of props that are so evident on the pantomime stage. These can hardly be worked on if several, or even just some, members of the cast are reading the lines and have their hands full of script.

The timing of pantomime moves is as complicated as that of a farce, and set pieces such as slosh scenes and chases require endless repetition in the rehearsal room to make sure they appear relaxed and easy on the stage. It might look a simple matter to the audience for someone to slip on a banana skin, somersault over a watering can, fall into a passing wheelbarrow and then be wheeled offstage. The whole episode may only take thirty seconds in performance. But the preparations need to be exact, for the safety of the actor as much as for the success of the gag.

FINAL REHEARSALS

Lighting and Sound Plotting
Lighting has a power akin to music to change a mood or enhance an emotion. It reacts on

---

Slipping on a Banana Skin!

The actor slips on a banana skin, falls over a watering can, tumbles into a passing wheelbarrow and is wheeled offstage. This simple comedy routine throws up many questions: none are particularly complicated, but they must be addressed if the gag is to get its laugh:

* How is the banana skin to be set in the right place, who will do it and when?
* Where should the watering-can be placed?
* Who is going to be holding the wheelbarrow at what angle, and through which entrances will it be wheeled on and off to appear to be just passing by?
* At what word in the script must the wheelbarrow's journey begin to make sure it will be at the right point on the stage for the actor to tumble into it?
* At what point in the script should the actor tread on the banana skin in order to fall into the wheelbarrow as it passes?
* Should the inside of the barrow, and possibly its top edges, be padded so the somersaulting actor does not injure himself?
* What sound effect will the band produce when he lands?

Despite all this careful preparation, the whole sequence has to look completely accidental, and only thorough rehearsal and good acting can do that.

Waiting for the cue in rehearsal. The children in the wings . . .

. . . and the dame preparing for his entrance.

our instincts and we are not always conscious of its effect. But we all know how much more positively people interact walking down the street on a sunny day, and the hunched intro-spectiveness engendered by grey drizzle.

The lighting designer will have planned certain effects and colours when reading the script and, after watching the show in a run-through or two, will have a good idea of the way he will light the show.

Throughout the rehearsal period the cue lines for sound effects and lighting changes will have been noted. Sound effects such as chiming bells or galloping horses will have been made ready and recorded onto a master tape, CD or minidisk. At the sound-plotting session, which may be combined with the technical rehearsal, the volume levels and cue lines will be set.

The director and lighting designer will see the lighting on the set in a rehearsal that does not usually involve the actors. It is essential to

Volunteers from the company 'walk the set' to check that the lights are correctly focused.

cajole some people into 'walking the set' while the lights are being focused and positioned, as it is almost impossible to judge if the actors are adequately lit without seeing the light on real, moving people. However well an actor performs, his work is wasted if the audience can't see it. The company may have seen the actors' expressions over and over again and be utterly familiar with the lines. But the audience have only one chance to see each moment, laugh at each joke or catch a fleeting expression. Their reactions will be slower and more muted if they cannot see. At the light-plotting session the level of light and the cue lines for all the changes will be decided, though many may need later adjustment.

Notes

After each of these rehearsals, as after every rehearsal, the director, musical director and choreographer will give the company notes on every point that needs further work. They may be as slight as an actor altering the stress on a

Sound operator and director setting light and volume levels in the auditorium at a plotting session.

single word or the sound operator upping the volume on a cockcrow. It may be a major change such as the insertion of a new page of dialogue, or a different costume for a quick-change that is not working fast enough. With luck and late-night work, these changes will be implemented and integrated into the performance before the first night.

Technical Terms

Theatre has a huge and peculiar vocabulary, much beloved by some initiates. Who else could guess that 'The Ghost walks on Fridays' means it is payday! Special terms have been avoided here wherever possible, unless they are so commonly used in theatres or rehearsals as to cause confusion if they are not understood in the same way by everyone.

Here is a small selection of those that are used by everyone, everyday in the theatre:

ASM – Assistant Stage Manager
Cloths – scenery painted on canvas suspended like a curtain
Downstage – the area of the stage nearest the audience
DSM – Deputy Stage Manager
Flats – panels of painted scenery
Flies – the area above the stage out of sight of the audience
Flying – lowering and raising scenery objects or people from the flies
Green room – actors' sitting room
MD – Musical Director
SM – Stage Manager
Stage left – the left-hand side of the stage from the actor's point of view
Stage right – the right-hand side of the stage from the actor's point of view
Tabs – curtains
Trap – a trapdoor to the area beneath the stage
Upstage – the area of the stage furthest from the audience
Wings – the sides of the stage area out of sight of the audience

THE SHOW OPENS

The director sees the pantomime afresh on the first night. It's the first time the audience are there to play their important role in the performance, and some of their reactions will be surprising and unexpected. He can do nothing on the first night but watch, hoping all goes well and taking notes for actors and technicians of places that could do with changes or more rehearsal. Most directors will see their show several times during the run and check that the performance is holding its shape. Pantomime, with its possibilities of improvisation and crosstalk with the audience can, during a long run, lose the shape and impetus that drives the story to a conclusion and

Actors and crew are given notes on the performance after the dress rehearsal.

holds the audience's attention from start to finish. The presence of the director in the audience will crisp up performances and remind

The youngest member of the company checks her costume in the mirror before her entrance.

everyone of the original intentions that they worked on in rehearsal. It is possible for the director to judge from a distance if all is going according to plan by asking to hear or see the show report that the stage manager of most theatres produces after every performance.

5 THE SET

By Colin Winslow

Traditionally, scenery for pantomime is pictorial, colourful and spectacular. In its heyday it featured a dazzling array of scene changes, and the most elaborate effects that could be devised. Long before the days of the cinema and computer-generated imagery, the scenery and special effects of the pantomime were the source of the greatest wonder and delight. These days, we may be working on a poorly equipped stage with a far from adequate budget. However, with a little ingenuity, it is still possible to produce some 'Oohs' and 'Aahs' from our audiences.

Nowadays, the storybook style of traditional pantomime design is a type of staging that we rarely see in any other form of production. You don't have to employ a pictorial style, of course; after all, innovation is also a well-established pantomime tradition. Pantomime does ask for some degree of spectacle and theatrical magic, but bear in mind that on a small stage and with a limited budget, a simple, but well-executed scene or special effect can carry as much 'punch' as a very elaborate and expensively produced scene on one of our biggest stages.

WHERE TO START?

It is a good idea to begin by tackling the technicalities. The most beautifully designed scene is useless if it won't fit on your stage, or cannot be set up in the time available. Acquire a decent scale plan of the stage. It should clearly show the proscenium, the edge of the stage, sets of flying lines (if available) and wing-space with any obstructions. Flying lines should be numbered, and the special winched sets designed for lighting equipment identified as 'LX 1', 'LX 2', and so on, numbering from the proscenium.

Sightlines

The seats at each end of the front row should be marked on the plan, and also the worst sightlines. Look how much of the stage can be seen by someone sitting at the right-hand end of the front row in the typical stage plan reproduced here: he or she can see the part of the stage between sightlines A-A, taking in most of the wing-space at one side of the stage, but not nearly so much on the other side. Note that the only area of the stage that can be seen by everyone in the audience is the area between the worst sightlines (B-B). From a careful study of your sightlines, you can work out where to place those really important features such as a king's throne or Cinderella's coach, which must be clearly seen by all.

Scale

The plan can be drawn at any scale you choose, but 1:25 is now the most popular scale. (If you still think in feet and inches instead of metres and centimetres, you may prefer 1:24 – or 'half an inch to one foot'.) This means that you can work out distances by measuring the plan, then multiplying by the scale factor to get the 'real' distance. For instance: at 1:25, a line 4cm long on the plan represents one metre in reality. A scale ruler will help here: it is simple to understand, and will do all the mathematics for you.

Deciding What Scenery Is Needed

There should be *no* delay between scenes, and the whole show should flow smoothly from

A snowy front-cloth in Red Riding Hood's forest. Photo: Rod Staines

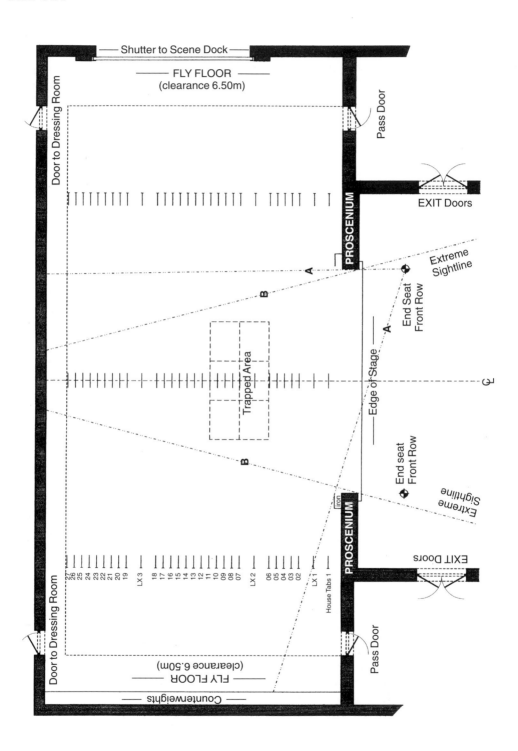

A typical stage plan.

one scene to another without a break. Even the slightest wait can be disastrous. The traditional pantomime format alternates 'front-cloth' and 'full-stage' scenes. This means that after a scene that takes up nearly all the stage, a painted cloth is lowered near the front of the stage for the following scene, so that the next full-stage scene can be set up (quietly!) behind it. Analyze the script: is the show constructed with this format in mind? How many front-cloths are needed? How many front-cloths can you accommodate? Or afford?

CLOTHS

Full-stage scenes may consist of a painted backcloth, wing pieces and/or 'cut-cloths', and, perhaps, one or more built, three-dimensional pieces (more on this later). It will be realized immediately that a theatre equipped with a flying system is at a tremendous advantage when designing pantomime. This means not only sets of lines with bars to hang your scenery on, but also sufficient height to fly them right out of sight. If you don't have a fly-ing system, it may be possible to rig a curtain track and draw painted scenes across the stage like a curtain (a 'traveller-cloth') or to rig one or two 'roller-cloths', which will roll down like a window blind.

Tumbling Cloths Some stages are equipped with a flying system but have insufficient height to fly cloths completely out of sight. In this case, it is sometimes possible to 'tumble' cloths between two sets of lines, thus halving the height of the cloth to be flown out.

Traveller-Cloth The traveller-cloth can sometimes be very effective when drawn across in full view of the audience: imagine Dick Whittington 'walking' to London in front of a very long traveller-cloth depicting the countryside through which he is passing, continuing across the stage and finally drawn off on the opposite side.

Front-Cloth Your front-cloth scenes will, by definition, take place near the front of the stage, but you should make sure there is enough space in front of the cloth for the

---

The Pantomime Experience

The interaction between performers and audience is an important element in pantomime. Actors frequently speak directly to the audience, inciting a vocal response, and will often physically invade the auditorium.

Most theatres have removable steps that can be set in place to provide access from auditorium to the stage, but the ingenious designer can often incorporate them into the overall design scheme. The false proscenium has a technical function, but can often be developed into a major decorative element, extending out of the theatre's proscenium into the auditorium, incorporating the access steps and providing an attractive and appropriate 'picture frame' for the action.

The 'pantomime experience' starts from the moment the audience enters the theatre: perhaps your design scheme could extend into the foyer, enhancing that sense of anticipatory excitement that we hope our audiences will experience on a visit to the pantomime.

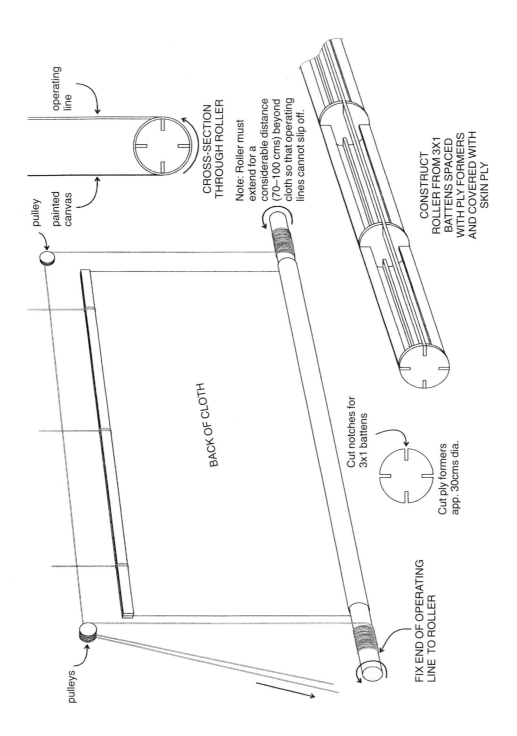

operating line

pulley

painted canvas

CROSS-SECTION THROUGH ROLLER

Note: Roller must extend for a considerable distance (70–100 cms) beyond cloth so that operating lines cannot slip off.

BACK OF CLOTH

Cut notches for 3x1 battens

Cut ply formers app. 30cms dia.

CONSTRUCT ROLLER FROM 3X1 BATTENS SPACED WITH PLY FORMERS AND COVERED WITH SKIN PLY

pulleys

FIX END OF OPERATING LINE TO ROLLER

Construction of a roller-cloth.

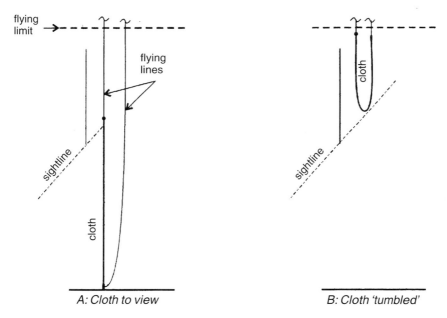

How a cloth 'tumbles'.

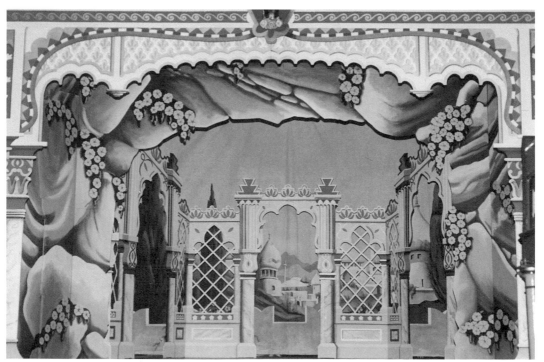

The false proscenium and decorative borders mask technical equipment. *Photo: Rod Staines*

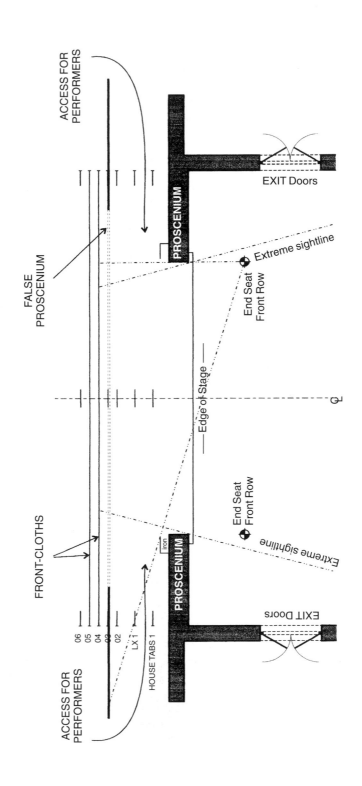

Stage plan with false proscenium and front-cloths.

necessary action. However, that annoying member of the audience who insists on sitting right at the end of the first row will be able to see the untidy edge of the painted cloth, and right past it into the wings where performers are waiting to enter. The solution is to place semi-permanent masking of some kind in just the right position to prevent this. This could be plain black flats or hung drapes, or some kind of special masking decorated in keeping with the theme of the show. You may have the same problem masking the tops of your front-cloths, in which case, consider joining together side masking and top masking to create a second proscenium inside the main one – usually referred to as a 'false proscenium'. This can often be a creative and attractive solution to a technical problem.

Full-Stage Sets

The most important scenes in your pantomime will probably take place in full-stage sets, consisting of a variety of scenic elements:

Backcloths At the very back of your scene there will almost certainly be a backcloth, sometimes just a painted 'sky' (or a lit cyclorama), which will serve as the background for several scenes. This may remain in position throughout the entire show. Of course, the backcloth will almost certainly not be wide enough to mask completely, so wing masking of some kind becomes necessary.

Wings Wings are basically just painted flats with a profiled edge to represent a tree, a house or some other appropriate feature. It is useful to make them as 'book-wings', which are folded in the middle like a book; they are then self-supporting and can also mask a much larger area than just a single flat.

Periaktoi A very useful trick here is to use the ancient device of periaktoi to support your wing pieces: three wing flats are fixed to a triangular base on castors forming a prism-shaped unit which can revolve on a central

Periaktoi in the model box
seen from above.

Periaktoi

Periaktoi are a very ancient theatrical device. They were first described in a treatise on architecture by the Roman writer Vetruvius (70–15BC) He described periaktoi, set into spaces in the theatre façade, which could be revolved to show different sides painted with backgrounds appropriate for comedy, tragedy or satire.

They were further developed and improved during the Renaissance and used by architect/designers of the seventeenth century, including the great Inigo Jones.

pivot fixed to the stage floor, thus enabling wings to be changed quickly, easily and noiselessly by simply revolving the whole unit.

Borders You will probably find that you also need some top masking to hide the unsightly tops of your backcloths and the lighting bars. This can, of course, consist of the normal black 'borders' that are usually part of the standard stage equipment. However, you may prefer to be more imaginative here, and design specially painted 'foliage', 'cloud' or 'architectural' borders as appropriate. You will need to refer to a stage section to work out the sizes and positions of your borders: this is a scale drawing that shows what you might see if the stage and auditorium had been sliced in half along the centreline and you were looking at the cut side of one of the severed halves. You can check 'vertical' sightlines from the front row in the same way that you checked the 'horizontal' sightlines on the plan, but now you can estimate what a member of the audience will see if he looks up.

Cut-cloth for Babes in the Wood, *Bristol Old Vic, 2000.*

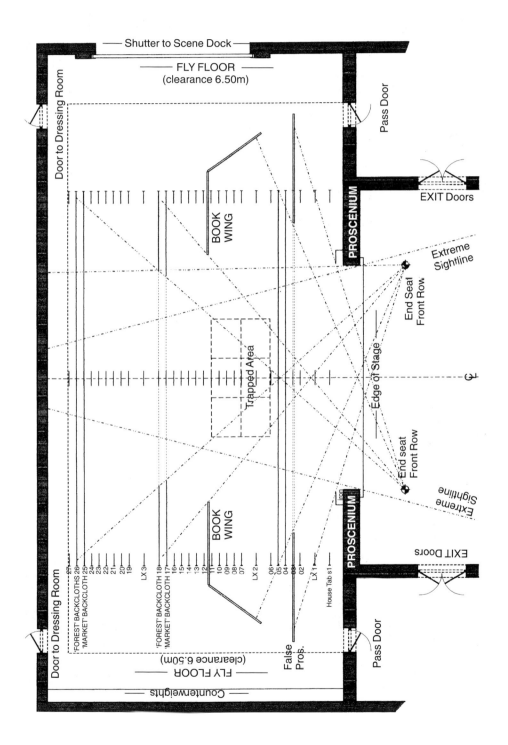

Stage plan with backcloths, cut-cloths and book-wings.

Cut-Cloths If you have flying facilities, a full-stage scene may incorporate a 'cut-cloth': here the side masking and top masking are dealt with at the same time by means of a painted cloth with a large area cut out of the centre to reveal part of the scene behind it.

You may find that a cut-cloth (or a painted border) needs some extra support to keep its shape – canvas trees can sometimes flop about in an alarming way! In this case, some fine net glued to the back will do the job and be virtually invisible from the auditorium. (Scenic suppliers sell nets designed specially for this.) Cut-cloths can be ingeniously designed so that they appear to be a natural and integral part of the total scene. They are particularly useful in a 'forest' or a 'cave' scene, or as an archway in a 'market' scene.

Mark all your cloths and wing pieces on the stage plan, showing clearly which sets of lines you intend to use. Examine the stage plan, which now includes a couple of back-cloths, cut-cloths (the cut-out areas marked with dashed lines) and book-wings marked for two full-stage scenes.

Draw all the sightlines from the end seats of the front row to check masking. Don't forget that the lighting designer also needs to plan where to hang lanterns, so you should confer at an early stage and resolve any possible clashes. Your scenery will look a lot better if it is effectively lit.

Built pieces Full-stage scenes are often enhanced by a change of level such as a staircase for Cinderella's ballroom or a grassy bank in the forest for the Babes in the Wood.

These can be built as 'trucks', that is, as a wheeled platform for ease of setting and removal. Use heavy-duty swivel castors, and don't forget to allow sufficient space under the truck to contain them and allow them to swivel. Your trucks will need to be securely fixed when in position. Elaborate brakes of various types are manufactured for this, but the cheapest method is probably the most secure: wooden wedges kicked underneath at strategic points, with a length of rope or hook attached so that they can be easily removed. Mark your trucks on the stage plan in on- and offstage

The train, a truck manipulated by the stage management, puffs onstage. Photo: Rod Staines

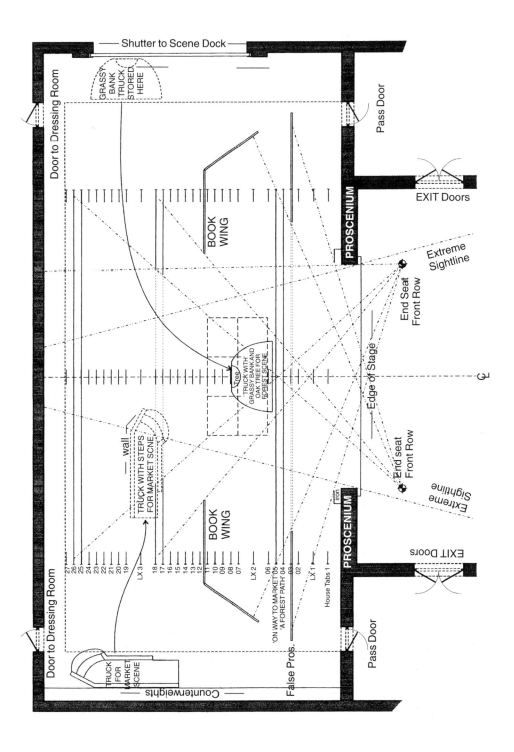

Stage plan showing positions of trucks.

positions, so that the stage manager can begin to plan the movement of 'traffic' during the performance.

We now have a stage plan with a false proscenium, two front-cloths and two full-stage scenes. As the plan grows in complexity, you may find you need to make separate plans for each scene.

Let's start to work on some of the more creative and imaginative aspects of the design.

PICTORIAL MATTERS

There's no getting away from it: it helps if you can draw. However, there are ways round it if you are unsure of your abilities. First of all, do

Treasure chest with the colour blocked in . . .

. . . and with the detail added.

some research. I strongly suggest looking at books of fairy tales by the great illustrators such as Arthur Rackham, Edmund Dulac or Maxfield Parrish. Some of the new children's books are also beautifully illustrated and can be a great source of inspiration.

You must, of course, be careful not to infringe copyright, but it is now a simple matter to manipulate a digital scan; to select, reproportion, re-group and otherwise change picture elements to produce an entirely new composition. If you don't have access to a computer you can do this by tracing and redrawing, but do try to maintain a consistent style.

Other avenues to explore are the Victorian toy theatre sheets published by Benjamin Pollock and still available in reproduction; or you might try to adopt a somewhat 'child-like' style – even consider asking a very young child (or a primary school class) to paint pictures for your scenes, then adjust for scale and proportion, and reproduce them as accurately as you can.

A painted cloth is, of its nature, flat. However, it is possible to make use of a few simple perspective tricks to give at least the illusion of depth.

Colour

Remember that all your work is going to be seen under coloured lighting: the lighting designer may choose to light a night scene with a bluish light, for example, and this will intensify any blue paint you use and tend to kill the reds. For this reason, it is often a good idea to limit the range of colours you use in a scene. A useful trick is to try to compose a scene without using one of the primary colours (red, yellow and blue) at all. If, for example, you omit red, then you are still left with a wide range of colours including yellow, blue and green, and all the tints and shades of these colours. You then have the opportunity to use the colour you have omitted to produce special emphasis where you feel it is needed. In pantomime our audience is usually treated to

An illusion of depth is painted on a flat back-cloth. Photo: Rod Staines

a succession of brightly coloured scenes and these are more effective if they are contrasted in their colour range, rather than using every colour available in every scene. (The 'Castle Corridor' front-cloth for *Jack and the Beanstalk* and the Act Drop for *Mother Goose* at Bristol Old Vic both have very restricted palettes.)

It helps if your coloured designs are produced at the same scale as your plans and other technical drawings.

Reproducing the Design

You now need to draw a square grid over your cloth designs. To preserve your original work either use a photocopy, or draw the grid onto a sheet of acetate and lay it over the design. The size of the squares will depend upon the amount of detail in your design, but 1cm is generally a good size. Next, draw the same grid on the scenery to be painted, but this time at full size. If your design is at a scale of 1:25 then each 1cm square on the design represents a 25cm square on the actual scenery. Working in imperial at a scale of 1:24, each ½ in square would represent a 1ft square.

Scenic suppliers sell various widths and grades of fireproofed canvas or calico and will make up the cloth to any size you require, adding the necessary fastenings and pocket hems for battens to keep the cloth hanging nice and flat. All seams should be *horizontal* so that the weight of the cloth itself will tend to pull them out and make them less visible.

The easiest way to paint a cloth is by attaching it to a vertical paint frame that can be raised or lowered through the paint-shop floor, so that any part of the cloth is readily accessible. However, unless you are very lucky you won't have access to one of these, and you will have to paint your cloths on the floor. Remember that scene canvas shrinks! You will need to fasten it down with tacks or staples placed fairly close together – about 10cm apart – to avoid distortion.

The best priming is still the old-fashioned mix of size and whiting. However, heavily diluted white emulsion paint is now a much simpler substitute. It sometimes helps to put a few drops of colour into your priming so that you can easily see any accidentally 'skipped' areas against the white canvas.

Front-cloth for Jack and the Beanstalk, *Bristol Old Vic, 1999.*

Some of this half-finished cloth is complete; the rest is sketched in and unpainted. Photo: Rod Staines

When the priming is thoroughly dry you can begin to mark out the grid you have placed over the design onto the cloth at full size. Begin with the vertical centreline and work outwards to each side. Horizontal lines start from the bottom edge of the cloth. A chalked snapline is a big help here.

With the grid in place, you can lightly sketch in your design. Use charcoal or chalk, and with the gridded design in your hand, mark out the detail in each square, comparing it to the equivalent square on the design.

Always use matt, water-soluble paints. The paints manufactured specially for scenic work are always better than the kind sold for interior decoration: the colours are more intense and lack the 'pastel' quality found in most domestic paints. Rosco make an excellent range of colours for scenic work: the pigments are very concentrated and can be mixed and diluted to a thin wash, thus producing the scenic equivalent of an artist's watercolours.

Painting details on the castle door.

It is usually best to start with the paler background colours – particularly if there is a large area of 'sky' – and work forward to the more intense and detailed foreground. Remember that no-one is going to be looking at your work as closely as you are when you are painting it. Try to keep it fresh and don't overwork it.

Don't forget to paint the edges of flats and built pieces: They will show, and it is a very tedious business to match them in later.

TRICKS AND TRANSFORMATIONS

Traditionally every pantomime has its 'transformation scene'. This is when, just for a few moments, the designer is allowed to take over the show. In *Jack and the Beanstalk* it happens when the beanstalk magically grows up to the sky; in *Cinderella* it is when the pumpkin is turned into a glittering coach for the trip to the ball; and in *Aladdin* it is when the Genie makes the cave of jewels vanish before our eyes. Victorian pantomimes contained very ingenious multiple transformations that were breathtaking to watch and required vast resources to produce. Today, our effects are generally much simpler affairs, but still employ some of the same techniques.

Periaktoi are a great help here. Wing pieces can be swiftly revolved to bring a second piece into view. They can also be arranged with several of them in a row, each side painted as part of a different scene. They can then be revolved to produce the same kind of effect that we sometimes see used in large advertisement sites, which seem to 'dissolve' from one design to another.

Cloths can, of course, be swiftly flown out or drawn aside to reveal another cloth behind, and trucks can be revolved to reveal a hidden side, or moved smoothly offstage by stage crew

A startling transformation on a small stage with very limited flying facilities.
Photos: Rod Staines

hidden behind them. A strategically placed pivot will cause a truck to move from one part of the stage to another as it revolves. Don't forget that lighting effects, pyrotechnic flashes and stage 'smoke' are all very effective aids in creating a truly magical transformation.

Gauzes

The most 'magical' effects are usually produced by means of painted 'gauzes'. These work rather like the sheer net curtains hanging at your window: during the day, when the light outside is brighter than the light in your room, from the street they appear to be opaque, but at night, when it is dark outside and the lights are switched on in your room, the balance of light is reversed and they appear to be transparent. The same principle applies even if the net curtain has a design printed on it.

Two types of gauze are in general use on stage: 'scenic' and 'sharkstooth'. Scenic gauze is useful for creating misty effects – but will never become completely opaque. For trans-

formation effects you need sharkstooth gauze. This is available from scenic suppliers in white, grey or black, and is usually up to nine metres wide. (Seams will show as black lines when the gauze becomes transparent.) Take care not to fill the weave of the gauze with paint: use no priming, and dilute the paint to a thin wash. Gauze will shrink and distort, so pin it out carefully to maintain its size and shape.

When the painted gauze drop is hanging in place on stage, and lit only from the front, it will appear as solid as any other painted drop. However, if you slowly bring up lights on a scene set behind the gauze and reduce the light from the front, it will gradually become completely transparent and your painted scene will 'magically' vanish.

When the gauze is in its opaque state, any movement behind it will tend to show through, so if it is essential to have people working behind it during the performance, you should hang some black masking curtains on a set of lines immediately behind the gauze – which can be removed just before the trans-

Technical Rehearsals

The designer's work is not over when the designs are complete. In many amateur or smaller professional companies the designer will often be expected to help with painting or building the scenery. When the actors begin to rehearse on stage with the actual scenery, the designer will need to supervise the technical operation of any special scenic effects.

For a transformation scene to be really effective, all the various elements need to be very carefully timed so that scenery, lighting, sound and action are all integrated into the total effect. It can take a long time and a good deal of effort to get everything working just right. For this reason, it is a good idea to ask for a special technical rehearsal to be arranged for any special effects, so that the crew can get them working as smoothly as possible, before the actors are introduced into the scene.

The designer should be sitting in the auditorium at these times to see the effect from the audience's point of view. Remember that the crew working onstage have no way to judge the total effect of their work. Your comments are important. Do not physically help the crew at rehearsal, unless you intend to do so at every performance.

formation. The gauze's opacity may be improved by lighting from a slight angle, avoiding light hitting it from directly in front and passing straight through the weave.

The painted gauze for *Mother Goose* was used behind a false proscenium as an Act Drop. A short prologue for Fairy Queen and Demon King took place in front of the gauze – then it slowly became transparent to reveal the scene set up behind, and was flown out unobtrusively when completely transparent, giving the impression that we had travelled 'through' the painted picture.

Black Light

This is really ultra-violet (UV) light produced by means of special bulbs (usually tubular) and more or less invisible. However, special paints or fabrics will fluoresce in brilliant colours when seen under ultra-violet light. Water-soluble UV paints are available from scenic suppliers. They work best when applied over a special white base paint, but any white base will do. Note that the paints do not necessarily fluoresce in the same colour as the pigment.

Because *only* UV-sensitive pigments are visible under black light, very magical effects can be obtained by using operators dressed in black moving fluorescent props or set pieces. It can be especially effective in an underwater scene (shoals of glowing fish), an enchanted forest (fluorescent butterflies), or a haunted castle (dancing skeletons).

Black-light effects do have limitations, however, and should be planned with care. For instance, they are really only effective when seen under UV light, with no ambient light. This means that actors' faces and hands will disappear, even if their costumes have been made from UV fabrics, and they will seem to be disconcertingly 'headless'. Special UV make-up has been developed, but its effect is usually crude and clown-like.

'Invisible' UV paint is also available. It is rather like a matt glaze and is hardly detectable under ordinary lighting, but glows brightly when seen under UV light. This can provide a really inexpensive substitute for a 'star-cloth': just paint tiny dots of 'invisible' UV paint all over a painted sky – I do it by pouring out a little of the paint onto a saucer and using the eraser on the end of a pencil to 'print' the stars. The stars will not be seen under normal lights, but will gradually appear as the stage lights dim for a night scene, allowing the UV lights to take over and produce a wonderful starry sky. You can make a moon appear in the same way.

Special effects never work properly the first time you try them – so allow as much time as you possibly can to rehearse and re-rehearse them to get them just right, and produce those gratifying 'Oohs' and 'Aahs'.

Colin Winslow is a stage designer with many years of professional experience. His work has been wide-ranging, from Shakespeare in Belgium to Ibsen in the Prairies; from ballet in London to the Edinburgh Military Tattoo in Washington, DC. He has designed many pantomimes throughout the UK.

He has been Head of Design for several theatres including the Redgrave Theatre in Farnham, the Royal Lyceum Theatre in Edinburgh, the Manitoba Theatre Center in Winnipeg and 'Ensemble' in Amsterdam.

He has taught stage design in many drama schools and universities in England, and is currently teaching and designing at the University of Alberta in Canada. He is the author of The Oberon Glossary of Theatrical Terms.

6 THE COSTUMES

antomime often relates a story of a time in the past. Its costume, however, behaves in a way that only the most post-modern production of a period play could stomach. Pantomime reality, which treats the most serious subjects with anarchic licence, takes extreme liberties with historical costume and we in the audience accept, enjoy and laugh at these liberties. The audience, even an audience of picky costume historians, would not mutter about a wrongly shaped corset or an inaccurate bonnet. Where but on a pantomime stage would you accept that the Lord Mayor of 15th-century London wore fishnet tights on elegant legs, the prettiest and most modern make-up in town and was, in fact, a vibrant young woman? When else might a Victorian chorus line make visual reference to a modern pop-group?

Tradition, ruling with an iron hand, has taught us that Robin Hood wears green. ('What! In that damp and muddy English forest?' 'Yes, always green, Lincoln green – never took it off.') And Kings and Queens wear crowns ('All the time? 'Yes, even in the bath.') And even children know that grandfathers wear nightcaps in bed, though how many centrally heated children today have seen their grandfather in a nightcap? The costume designer of a pantomime overrules these

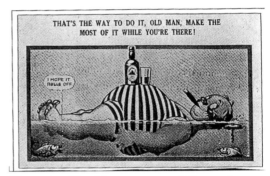

The striped bathing costume of the early 1900s which stands for a male bathing suit in all Panto-eras.

notions at his or her peril. They are a short cut to the audience understanding messages that we must convey quickly, and clearly, to all the men, women, boys and girls about character and plot.

RESEARCH

The costume is often a long way away from the realistic period costume demanded by naturalistic period plays. It can bear little relation to a historical past. A mediaeval lad might be dressed in fishnet tights, PVC hot pants and a velvet tunic with ruffles, rather than the rough wool tunic and baggy leggings of reality. Consequently, it might seem ridiculous to

85

begin a chapter on pantomime costume with the heading 'Research'. Nonetheless, this is where the designer begins, and it is the first act of the design process. Pantomime stories are folk tales, and can be translated to many different times and countries. Cinderella is French in France, Russian in Russia and English in England. The Babes in the Wood could be mediaeval lordlings or teenagers lost and sleeping rough in a doorway in Central London. It depends on the script.

It is impossible to direct the flights of design fancy necessitated by the particular exaggerations and simplifications of pantomime costume without a thorough knowledge of what the real people of the time were up to.

There are many excellent books on costume that will help you to visualize the clothes of the past. Illustrations in children's books, folk costume and national dress will nudge the imagination in a pantomime direction. But pantomime reality, while rooted in tradition and real life, behaves in a way of its own. Many of the characters are allowed to step outside the strictures inflicted by correct period costume. Boldly stated exaggerations of reality, or a combination of modern and period costume, create a style that is recognized by the audience as belonging to a particular period while retaining the familiar rules of the traditional pantomime characters. The secret lies in the underlying sense that allows us to believe such wild anomalies are in the characters we are dressing.

THE SCRIPT

The designer's imagination must follow the script to the land and time in which the characters live, and gather different types of information which can be slotted into three categories: the creative, the practical and the costume plot.

Creative Inspiration

The journey to a happy conclusion that forms the drive of a pantomime story is usually straightforward. But the urban or rural situation, the era, the social differences between the characters, and the colours and patterns that appear in the imagination are sparked by the first reading of the play. It is this reading that will jump-start the creative work of design. It will use the research you have done on the period as a springboard, but it is the story that makes you fly. The practical demands of pantomime design work, which are so fraught with technical demands, can bury this initial instinctive response under a pile of problems if it is not noted and guarded with care. Don't forget to be as funny, as romantic, as bold and as colourful as the script.

The Practical

The first of these practical considerations is the budget. The best ideas are useless if there is not enough money to make them happen. An idea that seems beyond the reach of the budget can often be pruned a little, or reshaped so that it can be used. The huge magic cloak that descends from the skies in billowing folds of silk may have to end up as an extra-large robe worn by an actor holding sticks with which he can swirl the cloak around. The effect will still be stunning. A positive and realistic attitude is a great help, as is the self-control to jettison an idea that you love but which does not help the story. The venue must be considered because it will affect both the distance from which the audience will see your costumes and the space the actors have to work in. Delicate detail must be carefully pointed with contrast if it is to

Exaggerations of Reality

The root. The Edwardian tweed suit and buff waistcoat of a country gentleman.

The developed costume. An overlarge check tweed with a bright yellow waistcoat.

Notice that the jacket has been cut shorter and wider and the knickerbockers more fully to create stockiness in the character. The pattern in the cloth and accessories has been enlarged in a cartoon style. Despite this the character, in both cases, gives an impression of a country gentleman.

show in a large theatre. And smaller points, which can be lost in a large venue, can prove delightful in a little theatre. Trapdoors, fly towers and other useful aids to magic changes are not always available; ingenuity has to take their place.

Costume Plot

An accurate and complete costume plot is essential. The careful plotting of quick-changes and doubling, costume props and tricks will avoid mistakes that could otherwise escape notice until the technical rehearsal, when it is discovered that a quick change cannot be performed in the time or space available. Timings and the script will change during rehearsals, but at least you will be prepared and the coat that must conceal a half-changed actor from the audience will have been designed, allowed for in the budget and made. A reliable costume plot, which has been steadily updated throughout rehearsals, can save hours of expensive frustration at the technical and dress rehearsals.

Role	Act 1 Scene i	Act 1 Scene ii	Act 1 Scene iii	Act 1 Scene iv
	The Forest	Continuous action. Forest lane front-cloth	West wing of castle.	Forest lane front-cloth
Robin	Pocket for acorns	As before		'Water' in hat
Sam	Travelling jacket; hat	Jacket off onstage	Pocket for catapult	
Janet	Travelling coat; hat; doll in identical costume.	Hat off onstage		
Nurse, the Dame	Bonnet; ridiculous bag for many props (divided pockets inside bag); shawl, glasses?	Trick pocket in knickers for chinking coins	Cloak and barmy mortar board	Quick change to outdoor 'flirting in forest' frock and hat; fan
Witch	Trick glove for smoke effect	Takes off shawl		Costume worn with unstiffened cloak for disappearing down trap; costume for double actor seen from back only

Part of a costume plot, showing the information a designer collects from the script before starting the drawings.

THE COSTUME TEAM

This, of course, varies enormously depending on the size and finances of the production but will consist of:

Designer (also, sometimes, the set and lighting designer) Responsible for inventing and creating the look of the costumes.

Supervisor Controls the costume budget; supports the designer's vision in choosing cloth, haberdashery, and so on, appropriate to design and budget; liaises between designers and makers; arranges fittings and makes sure they run smoothly and productively; chooses, in consultation with the designer, and arranges the hiring of costumes; answers questions from every direction; and, if they are good at their job, makes the costumes scram-

The costume supervisor's work is both organizational and practical.

ble off the drawing paper and onto the actor's body with the effortless ease of a magician!

Cutters Cut the cloth according to the designs.

Makers Make or alter the costumes.

Sometimes all these jobs are done by one person with an assistant or two, sometimes by one person in charge and some enthusiastic volunteer helpers. Sometimes there are extra workers such as make-up artists, mask makers, puppet makers and, often called for by the appearance of Daisy the Cow or the pantomime horse, animal skin makers.

Wardrobe Master or Mistress. A title still used to describe someone who does any or all of these jobs or, in big companies, takes care of the costumes during the run of the show.

COMMUNICATION

The costume designer must communicate with the rest of the creative team to make sure everyone's ideas are on the same track:

Directors Ascertain the way they envisage the general look of the show and any particular costume ideas that they would like incorporated into the design. Chart any tricks, changes or magic that the director may have

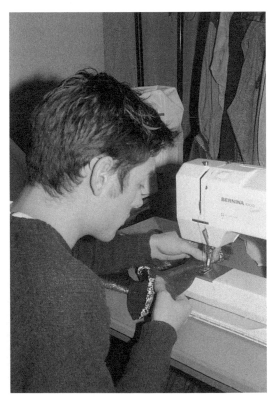

Though machine sewing is more usual, sometimes only hand sewing will create the right effect.

in mind which may not be apparent in the script reading.

Set designer This may, of course, be you as costume and set design often go together. Exchanges of ideas throughout the design process will make sure costumes and set work well together. See the designs and work knowing the background against which your costumes will move if the sets are hired, or designed before the costumes

Lighting designer The colours you use will be affected by the colour of the lighting. You will waste your time and money designing and making elaborate and subtle costumes for a scene that is so dimly lit that your careful work will not be visible to the audience or is lit to appear only in silhouette. Talk through each scene and discover the plans. Lighting designers have a magic power at their fingertips and can make your costumes look wonderful or dull as ditchwater at the flick of a switch.

Movement director or choreographer Actors have to move in your costumes and pantomime actors are rarely still on the stage. You will need to know about, and budget for, any special clothes or shoes that may be needed, for instance, to be worn for a tap routine or clog dance. It should be remembered that whatever the demands of the dance, pantomime is always active and actors must be able to move easily in the costumes in which they will spend so many hours.

Stage management team Much of the time your work may overlap with that of the stage management. Many pantomime props are a mixture of prop and costume, and there will be numerous bags, pouches and accessories on

Keeping Actors Happy in their Costumes

Actors must be as comfortable as possible. They dance, perform complicated physical routines, hare about the audience and act their socks off, while offstage they are often changing or belting around backstage to be in time and place for their next entrance. If you are tempted to skimp on making an actor comfortable, try wearing a pair of uncomfortable shoes and a shirt with tight armholes for a few hours and imagine whether you could do your best work in them.

Comfortable actors who can move freely and get out of their costumes easily sweat less (less washing for the wardrobe) and perform better.

the Tom Tiddler's ground that lies between prop and costume. Sort out who takes responsibility for what as early as possible but be prepared for change. Business with props will be developed in rehearsal, and the stage management team will keep you informed about the need and size of pockets and aprons, and so on. Ask if they will give you a list at the end of each day of any developments in rehearsal that concern the wardrobe.

Production manager Before anything can be designed, bought or made, you must be certain of how much you can spend, how long you will have to produce the costumes and the experience and availability of assistants. The different combinations of jobs within the costume department will affect the spending of the budget, but one person must have the overall responsibility for keeping track of the spending.

Actors Talking to an actor about the design and practicality of their costume will be time well spent. Actors know the moves they have to make onstage, the speed with which they will have to produce a prop from a pocket and whether their shoes or trousers will be practical to dance in. Actors can't see themselves, but always know what feels right; the balance between the two will work more successfully where good communication is established between the pantomime wardrobe and the cast.

Children Make sure children feel confident at fittings. Shy or nervous children do not always say that they are unhappy in their costume, and you don't find out until the fidget and wriggle at the dress rehearsal that they are being given a rash by their costume, or that their shoes are too tight. Great care should be taken at fittings to make sure the children are really comfortable and feel confident. It's easy for boys to feel silly in period clothes which they feel are girly; show them the show designs and point out that the men, as well as the boys, may be wearing frills and tights.

THE COSTUMES

We will assume for the purposes of this book that you are a company working on a limited budget in a small theatre, hall or arts centre. It is probable that the costumes you are working on will be a mixture of items already in stock in the theatre, items designed and made specially for the particular production, and outfits hired from a theatrical hire shop.

The person responsible for the way the cast look onstage, who we will refer to as the designer, though she may in fact be the wardrobe mistress, or in a very small company the stage manager, should always be present, or at least consulted, when decisions and choices are being made. It is easy, when communications are not good, for an outfit to be hired that is completely out of keeping with the rest of the costumes. Confusion in the costume department will confuse the audience and lessen their enjoyment of the play. The most important help costumes give to pantomime, apart from delighting the eye and making people laugh, is a clear, easily understood picture that gives the audience an immediate understanding of the characters.

Specially Designed Costumes

Every costume for every character should have a drawing with attached examples of cloth. The designer will know from the information in the costume plot if quick changes, secret pockets or particular accessories should be included. These drawings should be as informative as possible and may contain written as well as graphic information. It should be possible to give the drawing, the actor's measurements and the cloth to a maker and for them to be able to create a costume that is like the drawing.

Costumes 'Pulled' from Stock

Money and time can be saved when the theatre has a stock of costumes by selecting items from stock. Care should be taken to make sure that the 'pulled' costumes will sit comfortably onstage with those that are specially designed. In many cases they will have to be altered, added to, or perhaps dyed to fit in with the design of production.

Costumes Hired from a Specialist Source

It is not good enough to send off a list of requirements and measurements and take

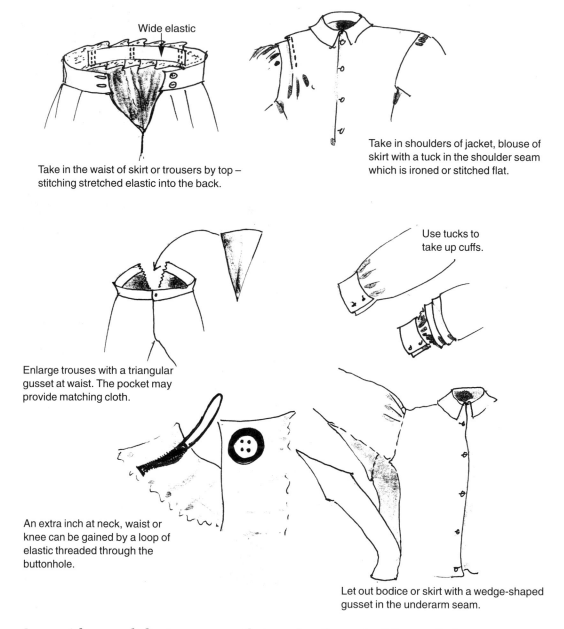

Wide elastic

Take in the waist of skirt or trousers by top –
stitching stretched elastic into the back.

Take in shoulders of jacket, blouse of
skirt with a tuck in the shoulder seam
which is ironed or stitched flat.

Use tucks to
take up cuffs.

Enlarge trouses with a triangular
gusset at waist. The pocket may
provide matching cloth.

An extra inch at neck, waist or
knee can be gained by a loop of
elastic threaded through the
buttonhole.

Let out bodice or skirt with a wedge-shaped
gusset in the underarm seam.

Some quick ways of altering costumes that speed up the work of the wardrobe.

what comes. The designer should choose from the hire stock to make sure he is getting what he wants. The costumes should be delivered in time to make alterations or changes if necessary, and to check that their quality will stand up to the wash and wear of pantomime vigour. Many hire firms send out forms that can be filled in with actors' measurements and requirements. With other, less formally run hire shops, the designer will rootle through the racks trying to find what he wants. The service and the quality of the costumes tend to be reflected in the price. Pantomime costumes are, of course, in great demand at Christmastime so it is wise to choose and book the costumes early. The firms will provide a form with a list of the measurements they require.

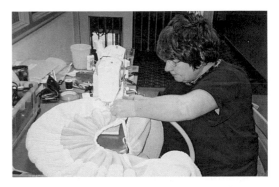

SOME STOCK PANTOMIME CHARACTERS AND SCENES, AND THEIR PARTICULAR COSTUME PROBLEMS

Pantomime is a sweaty business. Costumes must be able to be cleaned – preferably washed – quickly and easily. It is also energetic and the garments must be strong enough to survive considerable wear and tear. Slosh scenes, where food and water are chucked about, must be considered when choosing cloth for characters that are going to get covered with muck twice nightly!

Tights and stockings must be strong and springy enough to cope with kneeling down or knees-upping on the stage. The striped stockings worn by many Dames can be obtained from party and novelty shops that sell masks and wigs, and from theatrical suppliers. Some markets sell interesting thick, coloured stockings, though these are often too small for male feet. Coloured tubes of Lycra or other stretch

Pantomime costumes often call for more ingenuity than sewing. Here, a giant ruff is stiffened with a hula hoop and a skeleton bodged up with an old coat hanger and cardboard.

cloth can be sewn onto socks to make coloured stockings if boots will hide the join. Shoes must be suitable both for the look of the costume and for the vigorous action.

Wigs are a particular problem where budgets are small. The active life of Pantoland can mean that a wig that would still look good after a week in a straight play will look a wreck after the matinee of a pantomime. There will probably not be a wig-dresser to repair the damage. Address the problem early. Protect the wig on stage with fine invisible hairnets, offstage with a wig block (which can be improvised from an empty five-litre paint tin). If possible, use hats with hairpieces to avoid disrupting the wig with hat-changes throughout performances. Explain to actors the importance of treating their wigs with care. Pantomime wigs do not necessarily have to look like real hair, and imaginative solutions can create successful and often comic effects.

Different stock characters create particular problems.

The Dame

The most traditional of roles in the British pantomime cast. Dames come in all shapes and sizes and can be sophisticated society Madams or country washerwomen.

The costume of a traditional Dame begins, of course, with the bosom. This may be huge, high and pointed or a rounded pigeon-pouting chest, but it is always an exaggeration of reality and the Dame's boobs are a pantomime gag. Practically, they must be comfortable and washable and remain firmly in place. A large-size bra may be padded and perhaps widened at the back with elastic. It is often more successful to construct a false bosom on a close-fitting vest or bodice, possibly with petticoat attached. The padding should be made up of layers of washable wadding positioned between two bodice fronts like the filling in a sandwich. The wadding should be secured with stitches through all layers so that it cannot become misplaced and lumpy through the many washes and tumble-dries it will have to survive. Stockings can be kept up with garters, suspenders or tights with elastic braces. Avoid showing the skin as much as possible. Hairy chests, ankles and forearms spoil both the picture and the joke.

Dames wear bloomers: long and voluminous underpants gathered in at knee and waist. The Dame's pants are another stock pantomime joke and a good Dame can be roguishly and outrageously vulgar with these articles, which are in fact most decent. Shoes can be an expensive problem. They must be comfortable and easy to run and dance in. The button boots preferred by many Dames would have to come from a theatrical supplier. Lightweight men's ankle boots or large-size women's shoes are a cheaper alternative. And dance shops sell unusual male footwear.

The Dame will have more changes than any other member of the cast and they should be made as smooth-running and calm as possible to help the actor through the frenetic and exhausting activity of the performance. Her, or rather his, dresses (frocks in theatrical parlance) must be made with careful regard to the quick changes that are likely. Some actors feel safer if the fastenings are at the front so that they can manage their own changes. Others, if they have the choice, prefer to rely on the help of a dresser. It is wise to make it possible to wear the same underclothes, (petticoat, bloomers, and so on) under all Dames' costumes, and to make sure that the costumes can be taken off and put on without disturbing the wig and make-up. A Dame's make-up is usually an exaggerated and unrealistic parody of female make-up, with long eyelashes, painted eyebrows, rouged cheeks and an accentuated lip shape.

It is helpful for the actor if someone from the wardrobe can sit down quietly with him and go through the costume changes to compose a list of what accessories are to be worn with which dresses in what order throughout the play. Of course, if the Dame has a dresser this is unnecessary as they will have all the information to hand.

The variety of Dame's costume is huge but a few general points might be useful:

* Detail works better if it is clear and simple and does not overcomplicate the message of each costume.
* A heavy skirt may stay up better on a man with braces rather than a waistband.
* Hats and headdresses, always a feature of the Dame's costumes, are very often large, completely barmy and designed for comedy effect. They need to be secure on the head. A thick band of elastic under the chin disguised by a bow may prove the only answer if a hatpin won't hold them on.
* It can be better, particularly if the company does not have someone to restyle the wigs on a daily basis, to have a wig for each hat, or false hair attached to hats so that the wig does not have to be restyled in quick changes.
* Mittens can be made by cutting the fingers and thumb off gloves. They can also be made from thin stretch cloth tube or elastic lace caught together with a few stitches between thumb and forefinger, or from the leg of a pair of tights or stockings.

Actors who often play Dames sometimes travel with their own costumes and accessories, and their shoe or mittens collection can be a godsend to the wardrobe.

The Principal Boy

Today our hero, the Principal Boy, is often played by a young man. When played by an actress there should be no doubt in the minds

The Dame tests if she can dance without her hat falling off.

of the audience that he is a young woman dressed up as a boy. There is no flattening of the bosom or addition of a false beard and moustache to create confusion in the minds of the audience about the sex of this character. Despite the fact that we, unlike our Victorian ancestors, are quite used to seeing female legs on display, those legs remain the focus of attraction, rather than the bosom or the belly. The costume therefore, with its beautifully fitted tights, shorts or breeches, should draw attention to the legs, and the shoes or boots should be a flattering and very feminine version of the male boot or shoe. Principal Boys may stride but they do not clump. Their clothes may have a masculine slant but the cut and the fabrics are female.

The Villain

Pantomime baddies specialize in most varied villainy but have one thing in common – the audience must know they are bad immediately they see them and that they must be hissed and booed. The actor can be helped by the obvious clues in the colours and textures of his costume and the make-up he wears. The villain and the hero frequently come to blows. The more athletic of his dreadful deeds – the drawing of the sword, the quick footwork and the active pursuit – must be allowed for in the design of his costume.

Animals

Animal costumes, known as skins, are hot, unwieldy and uncomfortable. But the creatures – the cow, the goose or the beloved pantomime horse – delight the audience. Try to make sure the actors can take the heads of the costumes off quickly so that they can cool off and get some fresh air, even when the time offstage is short.

The Slosh Scene

This scene, where actors make an apparently chaotic mess with custard pies and flour, water and so on, must be prepared for by the wardrobe department well in advance. The real and messy props may not be used until the technical and dress rehearsal, and costumes may be ruined or at least in the sort of state where you have to waste valuable hours cleaning them ready for the performance. Ask the stage manager to let you know when the scene will be rehearsed, and watch the rehearsal taking careful note of where the mess lands. Provide aprons, overalls and hats as appropriate to both script and action. You may have to provide duplicate costumes for the next scene or performance if they cannot be cleaned in time.

The UV Light Scene

The ultra-violet light ('UV') scene is often included in pantomime, and in this case a test light should be rigged up near the wardrobe to make sure the effect is as planned. Any part of the costume or body of the actor that is not supposed to show in the light must be black. Make sure that gloves are well covered by sleeves, or sew the two together, and that socks and shoes are dark as well. Make hoods with gauze panels for eyeholes which tuck well into the neck of tops. Washing powder that contains a particular bleaching agent can leave a UV-sensitive residue; white underwear can show though black clothes under the light. Check all effects under a test light before you try them onstage.

LIFE IN THE WARDROBE

Fittings

Arrange the times of fittings with the stage manager. Try to give an idea of how long the fitting will take. In professional companies fittings are accounted for as part of the paid working day, so try to be accurate and well prepared for each fitting. Every hour in the fitting room is an hour less rehearsal time on stage. In non-professional or less formal companies well-organized fittings are a matter of courtesy rather than finance.

Children should be chaperoned at fittings. Ask direct questions such as 'Do those shoes feel tight?' rather than a vague 'Does that feel okay?' Ask children to run and jump in their costume fittings so that you can judge if the costumes fit well. Children who feel uncomfortable and awkward in costume will not be able to disguise the way they feel. They will fidget and twitch, pull down a skirt they feel is too short or scratch an itchy collar.

Make sure that girls' underwear, if it is likely to show, is part of the costume and kept at the theatre – don't rely on them remembering to wear the right underwear every day. The same is true of socks and tights. Little girls tend to fiddle with their hair, particularly when it falls over their faces. Invent a hairstyle that will prevent them hooking their hair behind their ears every few minutes. Make sure that both the children and their chaperone know what they will be wearing for each scene, and have rehearsed their quick changes.

Getting the Best out of Fittings

Use the time you are with the actor at fittings to solve problems in advance. Try out quick changes and any business that might have an effect on the costume. Check the position, size

Actors need time to play and experiment in their costumes at fittings.

and number of pockets; make sure the openings are big enough to get props out quickly, and that swords, guns and the like can be reached through the folds of the costume. Pockets sometimes need to be subdivided to make it easier for an actor to locate the right prop onstage. Check that hats stay on and do not obscure the actor's face from the audience or shade it from the light. Check that shoes are comfortable and don't slip. If actors have a lot of changes it is helpful to both them and you if you run through them all in sequence. Actors can accustom themselves to the order in which they wear their costumes and accessories, and you can see what's missing or what does not work or look as it should. Ask the

The washing machine, tumble drier and iron repair the damages of each performance.

actor to try out steps of dances in the costume shoes.

Go through any quick changes, preferably with someone reading the script to get the correct timing. It is much easier to rehearse a quick change or a transformation in the relative calm of the wardrobe than to try it out for the first time onstage. Use the time well to sort out any point that looks as if it might cause trouble later. There will be a huge rush of work as the opening night approaches, and the more you can get sorted out beforehand the more likely you are to be able to achieve the cool, calm and controlled appearance that will help the company have confidence in their appearance and your work.

Quick Changes

Pantomimes are riddled with quick changes and transformations. A rough timing can be taken at the reading of the script, but the stage manager will be able to give you an accurate timing when the relevant scenes of the script have been rehearsed. Find out if there is a dresser on hand or whether there is anyone with free time offstage who would help. Check that fastenings are as easy as possible and conveniently placed. Do not use zips: they are quick if they run smoothly but disastrous if they stick. Try the change out on a dummy or anyone you can persuade to check it out before the fitting. Time it with a stopwatch at the fitting and make sure the actor is confident that it will work. There are few things more damaging to an actor's nerves than panicking that he or she will have to go onstage half dressed.

Washing and Maintenance

Pantomime costumes lead a rough life. Most pantomimes are played twice or even three times a day. It is not always possible to provide doubles of costumes: dancing and general rushing about mean that they will be the sponges for pints of sweat. The delicate rosebud of a princess onstage will be wringing wet when she comes off it. If possible all actors, both male and female, should have an easily washed undergarment that can be changed between performances. Costumes must be made strongly enough to survive violent and repeated action. Seams that take strain should be double-stitched. Cloth that frays should be carefully finished with overlocking or tape, and armholes should be cut as generously as is practical. Shrink all fabrics that will be washed or tumble-dried by washing and tumbling them before you cut. A badly cut, uncomfortable costume will not wear as well as a well-cut comfortable one.

The Technical and Dress Rehearsals

All costumes should be ready in the appropriate dressing rooms before the technical rehearsal. But however well prepared you are, this first wearing of the costumes by the whole

---

The Invaluable List

Write down all the tasks, great and small, that have to be done to complete the costumes on a list. It gives you a view of how much work remains to be done. It means you can delegate jobs quickly and call for more help if you have to. And it gives you the satisfaction of crossing things off and feeling as if you are in control as the atmosphere in all departments of the theatre becomes more frenetic, and the scramble to complete the list in time begins.

---

company will produce a new, long list of jobs for the costume department. The hope is that every entry on this final list will be crossed out before the dress rehearsal, and that a calm and controlled atmosphere will hover over the wardrobe as the perfectly dressed actors stand in the wings waiting to go onstage for the first performance!

7   STAGE MANAGEMENT
By Ruth Staines

The stage manager of a large-scale commercial pantomime may be able to summon the electrics department to rig the lights, phone the property workshop to have an Aladdin's lamp made or ask a carpenter to cut a letterbox in a door so that another character may spy on the Dame. But small budgets mean small teams. Forget ideas of the deputy stage manager sitting in the prompt corner calling the actors for their entrances and cueing the fly men and the lighting, sound and pyrotechnics operators, while her team of assistant stage managers sets up the props tables and attends to the actors' every whim. The stage management team of a small-scale pantomime must be multi-skilled.

THE TEAM

Stage Management

The roles of stage manager and production manager may well be one and the same, or at least overlap. The DSM, who runs the rehearsals, is the most likely person to know the structure of the show and therefore to know where the cues come. She may well operate the lighting desk and audio players and, if she has three hands, the follow-spot as well! The ASM in the back end of the cow has to be able to rig lights, make props and shift the scenery. The stage manager will be responsible for the logistics of getting the show running smoothly, as well as being part of the crew herself. She will have to ensure that the scene change taking place when the cow is on the stage can be managed without the ASM who is otherwise engaged being the back legs.

Production Management

The production manager is the facilitator for the show, has control of the budget and ensures that the needs of all departments are met. Each department will be allocated a budget and a timescale, and given help and advice about suppliers, premises and Health and Safety requirements. She will find specialist suppliers: animal-skin makers for the goose in *Mother Goose*; a firm to enable Sinbad to fly off with the roc; a sound company to put the sound of a growing beanstalk onto disc. She may be responsible for employing, preparing contracts for and paying the set builder, costume maker or lighting designer, and possibly finding assistants for them if necessary. She will find premises for them to work in, and when the production moves into the venue will arrange space and facilities for all departments as well as rehearsal spaces for actors and musicians. She will organize the running budget for the show so that the costumes may

Rigging the set or running the sound and light cues are all in the day's work for the DSM.

be laundered and mended, food consumed onstage purchased, slosh prepared and running repairs made to the set, costumes, props and equipment.

REHEARSALS

Organization of Rehearsal Space

Organization of rehearsals is one of the most important aspects of stage-managing a pan-tomime. Unlike a 'straight' play, there can be several scenes in rehearsal at the same time. While the director rehearses dialogue scenes with the principals, the musical director can rehearse musical numbers with the chorus and the choreographer can put the children through their paces. And when any members of the cast are free, the costume department will want to see them for costume fittings. This

Health and Safety

Everyone in a theatre company must take responsibility for a safe working environment. This may mean using water-based paints where possible for scenery, or using a protective mask and working in a well-ventilated area when painting with solvent-based paints. Address anything that might present a hazard: ensure there is a rail around raised surfaces, or if this is impossible, warn actors and crew of the risk and ensure plenty of rehearsal so that everyone is aware of the possibility of falling or tripping. Risk assessments must be undertaken when the production is being planned.

Take the example of a theatrical flash – almost essential for a Cinderella transformation. The artistic decision will probably be that it is vital, but arrangements must be made to make it safe as well as spectacular. Use a flash cartridge system, with an electronic detonator, according to the manufacturer's instructions. Ensure that the set is flame-retardant, that actors in the scene are positioned well away and that the operator can see the cartridge as he fires it. All pyrotechnics can be dangerous and their use may be banned in some theatres. When the hazard is under control you can marvel at the gasps of amazement as Cinderella is magically prepared for the ball rather than going up in smoke!

Note that an important part of health and safety legislation concerns keeping records of your risk assessments, electrical testing and safety checks. In this way, you can show that care has been taken to avoid accidents and keep cast, crew and audience as safe as possible. It is worth checking legislation locally, as this can vary from country to country, and even from area to area.

is a juggling act between directors, actors, available spaces (especially if they are outside the performance venue) and the availability of necessary equipment such as pianos and keyboards. But it is vital to the smooth preparations for a pantomime, which is in effect a complex musical production, that no space or time is ever wasted.

Before the cast arrives, the floor of the rehearsal room must be marked out with the set plan drawn in PVC tape on the floor, using different-coloured tape for different scenes. The designer will have provided plans and drawings to scale. If the rehearsal space is smaller than the stage, important parts of the set like doorways and other entrances must be represented, together with furniture; using chairs, tables, and so on, from the start of rehearsals will save a lot of time when the actors get on to the set. A chair can stand in for Cinderella's coach, Jack's beanstalk or the Beast's rose-bush, so that actors can rehearse speaking their lines while having to negotiate sitting, climbing and the like.

Keeping the Script Up to Date

Pantomimes are unique in that even if the director is using an existing script, he and the actors may well wish to add their own words, songs or scenes. If the script has been specially written, the writer may well be present at rehearsals, and will often rewrite lines in conjunction with the directors and actors. In either case, changes to the script will have to be carefully recorded, and reprinted if necessary.

Communication

Communication during the rehearsal period is vital: this can be achieved via a central notice-board for rehearsal schedules, costume fittings and so on. Stage management should reinforce this by constantly checking in person that all departments have the information they require as the production progresses.

'On the Book'

The stage manager will need a large notebook in order to make notes of props to be bought, borrowed, hired or made. He will also record any lighting ideas such as the position of a spot for a solo, the necessity for a night scene or a follow-spot to pass on to the lighting designer. The sound department will need to know about effects, such as the sound of a growing beanstalk, that may be played from a

Department	Act/Scene	Notes
Costume	1.i	The Dame's bag needs pockets inside for lipstick and powder-puff.
Props	2.ii	The bucket for the firewood needs to be smaller to fit on the truck.
Props	2.iii	Confetti in baskets is required for this scene.
Stage management,	2.iii	There needs to be a hook above the mantelpiece on the stage left truck to hang the bucket.
Sound	2.v	Owl call.

Typical report noting the day's new information for each department.

Keeping the Company Informed

Care must be taken to ensure that script changes are given to everyone involved in the production. Obviously the cast, director and stage-management team, but also the wardrobe department, lighting designer, children's chaperone and front of house manager must be kept informed. It is all too easy to forget this last person – a live stage show is nothing without an audience, and the front of house staff are there to look after the audience. If they know exactly what is going on onstage, they will be prepared for possible exits of small children, and will be able to have all pre-ordered drinks ready in the bar for the interval.

minidisk or CD and effects played live by the band (maybe the fairy godmother's magic music!); there are also sounds created in the wings by stage management like the knock at the door before Prince Charming enters Cinderella's kitchen.

When rehearsals are under way the stage manager must take careful note of the director's blockings. These will be drawn in pencil on a blank sheet of paper opposite the relevant lines in the script. They will serve to remind the director of what he decided at a rehearsal, which may have taken place some days previously, and to enable the stage manager to take rehearsals while the director is watching a musical rehearsal, talking to the set designer or looking at costumes. Ultimately 'the book' will be the production manual. It is the final version of the script, and the precise moment for every cue for lights, sound, effects, scene changes and actors' calls is noted exactly where it occurs. Each cue has a stand-by warning so that everyone will be in position before the cue occurs.

Stand-In Props, Costumes and Furniture

By their very nature, pantomime props and costumes are larger than life, and therefore not the sort of things that actors would use or wear in the normal course of events. It is vital that they use and wear anything that they may find difficult to manoeuvre as early as possible in rehearsal. The real items may well be under construction, but it is not difficult to find substitutes. So, for example, the Dame must be offered a selection of bags in which to keep outlandish props that may be the subjects of appalling jokes. It is impossible to list what such props might be; they depend on the imagination of the writer, director and actor. They could include such delights as a sink plunger, a banana, a pair of giant bloomers – all items that a Dame could make much of. The DSM on the book will give a daily list of such props to the ASMs to find. She will also alert the wardrobe to the size and quantity of pockets needed in the Dame's dresses or apron – they may need to be small to hold a hanky or a coin, or ridiculously large to hold, say, a rubber turkey or a lavatory brush.

Other characters may require walking sticks or umbrellas – lethal weapons if not rehearsed carefully, and especially in the hands of children! Such items may well be part of a dance, so the choreographer will want the dancers to have, perhaps, broom handles cut to the required length. Some substitute will be needed for Aladdin's lamp, Cinderella's broom, Jack's axe, Little Red Riding Hood's basket: however good actors are at miming, it will save much time at the technical rehearsal if they know exactly what to do with their props. They need to know where to collect them and how they get rid of them, or a kettle may turn up in a forest! Tables and chairs are easy to find and should always be used in rehearsals if the

103

ASMs making props.

scene requires them. The actors should get used to where they are to sit and where to place their props.

As the props are being made, they will get to a half-way stage when the actors can try them out. Are they easy to handle? Do they stand up when put down quickly? Are they strong enough for the use they are going to get? If a character has to slam a mug hard down on a table, it should be unbreakable plastic rather than glass or china: cheap ones may be bought and painted, or made from papier mâché if there is time. A rose to be plucked night after night from a bush should be sewn fabric rather than glued paper, unless stage management is prepared for lengthy repairs! There is no point in painting a prop beautifully if it has to be altered after being tried out in rehearsal.

The same principles apply to rehearsal costumes. In particular actors, such as the Dame, who are called upon to wear long skirts, will at least need a sheet or curtain tied round their waist so they can learn how to handle it and not get it tied up in the set. Again, the choreographer will need costumes with cloaks, tails, trains and anything else that might be awkward, at an early stage. The SM must remind director and cast that anyone in an animal or other padded costume will need extra space allowed round them on the set.

Schedules

With so many things to rehearse in a short time, the best possible use must be made of the available spaces. The director may suggest an initial schedule well in advance of rehearsals, but it is inevitable that this will change. Some scenes will prove simpler to stage than others, some actors will find certain pieces harder than others, the writer may wish to rewrite, and the comic scenes will need to be worked out. So at the end of each day the SM will, in consultation with the director, produce a schedule for the following day to let each actor know when and where he will be required. He may rehearse a words-only scene with the director, have a session with the musical director on a solo number, and then join the whole cast to rehearse the dance finale with the choreographer. The stage manager must dovetail all these requirements and keep the whole production team informed as to what is going on where, so that as many problems as possible can be ironed out before the technical rehearsal.

SET BUILDING

Some simple set building may come within the remit of stage management. In any case the stage or production manager must be familiar with the designer's working drawings so that they can oversee the work of the carpenter, and ensure that the set will not only fit on the stage, but that it will also fit into the transport from workshop to venue, and through the access doors onto the stage. It should be light enough to be handled comfortably by the stage crew.

Translating and Checking the Plans

The pencil drawings may dovetail perfectly together on the plans, but in a transformation scene, when the set may be required to move in full view, is there enough space for everything to move easily? Is there enough room in the wings? If Cinderella's kitchen sticks on the rest of the set when it is moving aside to reveal the pony and coach the illusion is shattered. Is there room to get round doors easily when Widow Twankey chases her lazy son Aladdin? The SM must either consult with the carpenter and designer and alter the plans before the set is built, or be prepared for alteration during the fit-up. Time spent on the stage with the plans, carefully measuring up how each part of the set will fit, especially in a small venue, can save hours of heartache at the technical rehearsals.

Flats

Flats may be most simply built from thin plywood glued and stapled onto a timber frame. The plywood can overhang onto the onstage side, and be profiled – the shape of trees, houses, ships and castles can be cut out. But beware of sharp profiles that trap the unwary actor: the medieval sleeves of the Sheriff of Nottingham may well break the branches of Sherwood Forest! If it is necessary to have some projecting shapes – perhaps mouldings, ivy or flowers – strengthen them with a piece of batten or second layer of ply.

Cloths

Transformations will have been specially designed to take place in full view of the audi-

The set arrives at the theatre.

ence, with a little help from flashes, blackouts, smoke and lighting effects. It is likely that most of the other pantomime set changes will take place behind cloths, often 'on the road to somewhere', where we meet Jack taking the cow to market, Prince Charming on his hunt for Cinderella and Dick Whittington off to London to seek his fortune. Cloths may be flown, in venues that have the necessary facilities, drawn on a tab track or, if they must be kept out of the way and there is no height for flying, rolled or tumbled. They may be made of canvas, calico, sheeting, or gauze, depending on the effect required and the budget.

PROPS

Pantomime props can be a source of both endless fun and eternal head scratching. Just as the characters are larger than life, so must the props be. Ideally they should be linked into the style of the overall design. This does not necessarily mean having pieces of furniture expensively made: a table of a suitable size can be covered in fabric provided by the wardrobe, to tie in with the costumes, or with fabric painted in the style of the set. This may well be useful to hide a shelf with other props, perhaps the slosh for a kitchen scene. Chairs can be painted and reupholstered. Stands, for example to place the

Positioning a 'kitchen wall' truck on the set.

Attaching a tab to a track with snap-hooks onto runners.

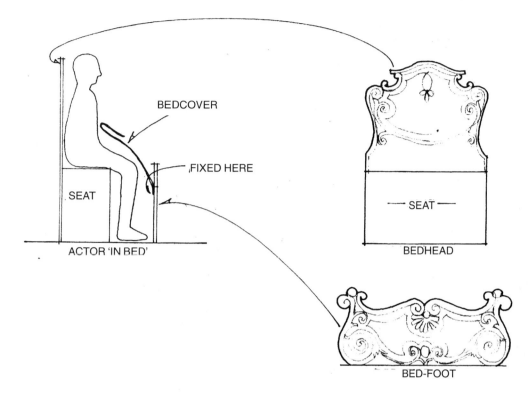

BEDCOVER

FIXED HERE

SEAT

ACTOR 'IN BED'

SEAT

BEDHEAD

BED-FOOT

The construction of a 'short bed'. It must be set facing the audience to be effective.

A 'short bed' on stage. Photo: Rod Staines

Giant's harp on, can be simply made but decoratively painted. Use a little lateral thinking when large items are required on a small stage: a short bed may be made by attaching a seat to the headboard and leaving a space just big enough for the actor's legs to fit between the seat and the end of the bed. With a cover over the lap, this gives the appearance of someone in bed.

Large Props

Furniture may have to be specially built to tie in with the set design. A table may need to be a particular size to fit in the available space, or be of an exaggerated scale for a Giant's castle. The construction can be simple, but must be stable and strong.

Sculptures may be carved from flame-retardant polystyrene, either with a hot wire cutter or a very sharp knife. It may be sanded with sandpaper or a surform, and is then best covered with flame-retardant muslin painted on with white emulsion paint, which will strengthen it and provide a suitable surface for painting. A pumpkin can be made this way. Of course the material is very light so if it is to represent stone or metal it must be fixed either to the set or to a heavy base. Remember that polystyrene will be melted by solvent-based glues, and when it is being cut or sanded the fragments will cling to everything. A useful tip is have a vacuum cleaner beside you as you work, so that you can clean up as you go and not leave an annoying trail when you move.

The pony drawing Cinderella's coach will fall into the category of large props! If the budget is large enough, specially trained ponies complete with coach and handler may be hired. If the budget will not run to this, a pony may be found which is quite used to unusual situations, goes into its owner's house, and up and down steps. Quiet and calm time must be allowed for the pony before the technical rehearsal, to make sure it is not frightened by any of the elements of the scene. For safety's sake it is better not to attach it to the coach, which can be pushed by footmen. Always have a bucket of sawdust to hand, for emergencies! Suggest to the director that there is as much noise as possible on stage or from the orchestra while the pony is getting into position – obvious hoof beats tend to destroy the illusion of the Fairy Godmother's magic!

The list of possible props in pantomimes is endless. They can be humorous, such as the Wicked Sea Captain's cat-o'-nine-tails that is in fact a soft toy cat with nine tails; surreal, such as a shark appearing in a forest; or practical, such as bows and arrows for Robin Hood and His Merry Men.

Weapons

Safety is an important consideration with all weapons, and the relevant safety documents should be consulted for up-to-date information. It may be possible to use toy bows and arrows with rubber tips, which will land safely on a suitable surface when fired from a short

---

Breaking Crockery

When something is required to break it often doesn't! It is as well to try to contain the plates that smash in something like a galvanized bath, as the pieces will be very sharp. A character such as Buttons will have to be instructed to clear up as much as possible, and it will be up to stage management to clear the stage thoroughly before the pony comes on! Stage weights can be placed into the container to encourage breakage.

3. Splitting it in half to insert the spit.

1. Cutting the polystyrene to rough shape with a kitchen knife.

2. Filing it smooth with a surform.

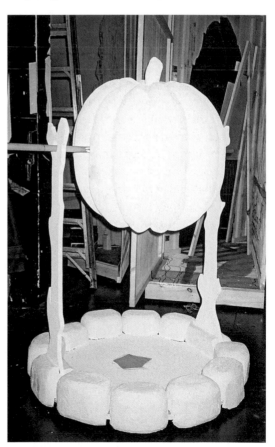

4. Pumpkin on spit ready for painting.

Making a giant pumpkin to turn into Cinderella's coach or roast on Robin Hood's spit. It will be covered with muslin and painted.

distance. Some regulations may allow real bows and arrows to be used, with professional tuition for the actors concerned, if the rest of the cast has been blocked to stand well away from the target. For an actor to hit the bull's-eye, a target needs to be made with a spring-loaded arrow hinged on the centre, which may be released at the appropriate moment by a Stage Manager behind it (the target must be placed on a stand large enough to hide a member of the stage crew.)

Other likely weapons are various types of swords and knives for fights between Dick Whittington and the pirates, between Ali Baba and the forty thieves, and between many other heroes and villains. Unless there is plenty of room on stage and the fights are choreographed by a professional fight director, it is best to play safe and use weapons of cut-out plywood or even foam rubber.

A Dame may well have a 'bopper' on her apron pocket or a bag with which to whack other characters or even members of the audience! In this case the bopper must be made entirely of foam rubber, covered in fabric to stop the foam tearing. The bopper may take the shape of a giant spoon, cosh or club. The foam can be cut with a very sharp blade.

An actor testing the weight of a blunderbuss in the rehearsal room. Current firearm regulations should be consulted before using any firearms of realistic appearance.

The ASM makes flintlock pistols from foam rubber, calico and paint.

Similarly a foam rubber hammer may be required for jokes such as 'I'll hold the stake, and when I nod my head, hit it!'

Classic Props

These must include the rat in *Dick Whittington*, Aladdin's lamp and the Beast's rose. A rat built on the base of a radio-controlled car might be used, provided that there is a skilled operator available and that it is not affected by other electronic equipment such as lighting desks! Otherwise it could run on a nylon line, but this must be carefully placed during the scene before, and removed afterwards. If neither of these is practical, it may be possible to make a comic 'soft toy' rat, and push and pull it on and off the stage with a stick, making a comic feature out of the silly-looking creature. The success of this method will depend on the skill of the scriptwriter in writing suitable lines, and of the director fitting it into the whole style of the show.

Aladdin's lamp may be bought in party or toy shops, or hired or made. The simplest and safest material is papier mâché, which requires time and patience to produce a really strong and well-finished prop. The layers of absorbent paper and glue can be laid over the article, provided it is not too precious, cut in half to remove when it is dry, and the two halves stuck together. The best finish requires a negative mould (a plaster cast needs to be taken of the object), and then decoration and paint can be applied. If a lamp can be made in a non-flammable material, a battery and switch may be built into it to set off a small pyrotechnic device (available from specialist suppliers) when the lamp is rubbed, enhancing the magic.

It is now easy to find realistic artificial plants, from single blooms to whole trees. The Beast's rose is, therefore, a relatively simple affair. If the script calls for the rose to be plucked from a bush, it is easy enough to drill a hole in the end of a branch (ensuring it is hidden amongst leaves) and insert the stem. If the rose needs to grow, it is helpful if there is a trapdoor in the stage. One of the crew can be positioned under it, and gently push the rose upwards through a piece of plastic pipe, which will be concealed behind the pot containing the bush. For the rose to lose its petals and die, and thus seal the Beast's fate, you will need two identical roses with the stems cut to the same length. One is the full bloom. The other, the one which loses its petals on stage, must have all its petals removed until only the stamen remains. Attach fishing line to single petals, thread this through the stamen and stick the other end on the stem with Blu-Tack. With careful rehearsal, the actor can release the Blu-Tack and the petals will drop. You will probably need to weight the petals slightly by sandwiching two together with a Blu-Tack filling.

Animated Props

Careful thought must be given to props such as beanstalks and giants. Consider skills and resources. The director may imagine a three-dimensional growing beanstalk, with complicated computerized motors and tendrils twining everywhere, but unless this can be made to work perfectly it is much better to stick to something simpler, cheaper and more foolproof. With the right acting from an astonished Jack, and atmospheric sounds and music, a beanstalk made of pieces of plywood covered with canvas or calico will look as though it is magically growing.

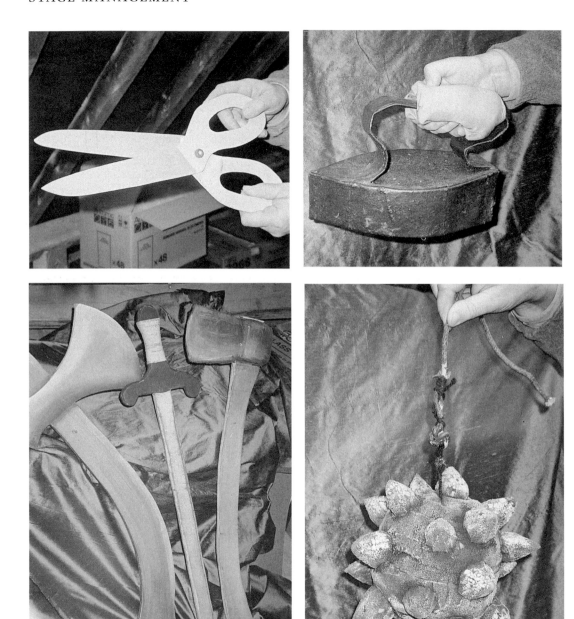

Props for pantomime are often oversized, lighter and simplified versions of the real thing.

Props for Audience Participation

One important element of pantomime is audience participation. This must of course be done safely and cleanly! A character with a bucket of (apparently) water, or worse, threatens to throw the contents over the audience; either the character will stop at the last minute, or the bucket will contain something innocuous, like confetti, torn paper, or long streamers attached to the base of the bucket.

Sometimes a prop may need to be planted in the audience. The cooperation of the front of house staff should be enlisted to check that the prop has not been moved and that they can be ready with a duplicate prop in an emergency. They should also be involved when sweets are thrown, having a few extra sweets to distribute to distraught youngsters who do not get any. The sweets themselves must be chosen carefully. They should be wrapped for hygiene – as many are bound to land on the floor – and as soft as possible, and the actors must be warned to throw gently underarm.

Audience members' birthdays, and mentions of school parties and societies, are always popular. Stage management must arrange for the actor, often the Dame, to receive the information from front of house before the start of the show if possible. Names should be written clearly, particularly if the Dame normally wears spectacles offstage, and any tricky pronunciations explained.

Slosh Scenes

The 'slosh' scene is a highlight of pantomime. However, as with special effects, it is better to omit the scene completely rather than make a half-hearted attempt at it. The scene is usually set in the kitchen, and the mess is created by a recipe going hilariously wrong! The Dame will attempt to bake a cake and her assistant –

Simple Simon, Buttons or whoever – ensures that it ends in a disaster such as an explosion or the mixture going over someone's face. If the stage is big enough, the mess can be contained on a specially prepared set, with washable paintwork and floor cloth. Costumes must also be washable, and dressers must be available with clean garments. In this case, flour, water, eggs, shaving foam – anything goes, so long as water is kept away from electrics and consideration given to what might go in the actors' eyes. But if the scenery is to appear later in the show, the actors may well have to clear up after themselves. Nothing slippery must be left on the floor, no obstacles to stop the rats running, and remember that dried egg white will definitely not come off the curtains, to say nothing of the audience!

Custard Pie Recipe

Actors who have had slosh in their face before may well have a favourite recipe. Here is one which works. Squeeze about 30cm (1ft) of lather shaving cream from its tube into 30ml (2tbs) of water and whisk with an egg whisk until it is a pile of foam. It can be coloured with a food colouring or water; it takes much less colour than you would think to tint a big pile of foam. This foam will stick to an upright surface (or face) and can be turned upside-down without dropping off. It retains its frothiness for plenty of time. It has enough strength to be able to support a removable addition (a circle of candles stuck on a backing, a lightweight prop banana) above the froth. The foam can sting the eyes, so wipe it off the eyelids before you open your eyes. Test any colour before you use it to make sure it doesn't stain. The foam washes off costumes, set and actor with ease, and doesn't get smelly.

113

Props during Production

It is one of stage management's most important jobs to organize the props during the run of the show. Some, like the Giant's harp and golden egg-laying chicken, will be arranged on the set by the crew. Those to be taken on by the actors must be put on tables placed in appropriate positions at the sides of the stage, unless the actors prefer to have them in their dressing rooms before the start of the show. In either case, stage management must check the presence and position of every prop before the start of each show. A missing rose on a bush, or the Dame's bag on the wrong side of the stage, can cause embarrassing moments of the sort that actors should not have to deal with.

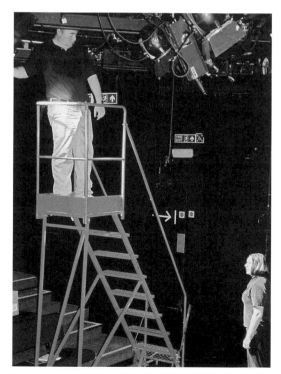

Rigging lights from the access tower.
Photo: Charlotte Cunningham

FIT UP

This is the moment when the production takes over the stage completely. If the set has been built *in situ*, possibly by the stage management team, time and money will have been saved as there will be no transport costs and no worry as to whether the individual pieces will fit through the access doors. If the set has been built by an outside contractor, arrangements must be made either for the builder to deliver the set, or for a van of a suitable size to be hired to move it from storage to the venue. Try, wherever possible, to have the builder present at the fit up, as he will probably have fitted each scene up in his workshop, and so will know exactly what fits to where; or if he has not, he will have prepared the necessary fixtures and fittings such as brackets, hinges and door furniture.

Pantomime is by its very nature a complex production, and the fit up and rigging of the lights and sound in the limited amount of time that is probably available must be organized with care: have a planning meeting beforehand with all the relevant staff. It is easier to rig lights above the set before the set is in place. Then, once the floor has been marked with coloured electrical tape according to the working drawings, it can be decided which parts of the set to put together first, especially if space is a constraint. It is no good putting up a run of permanently fixed portals (archways across the width of the stage) if there is then no room to place a tower or ladder between them to rig tab tracks and roll cloths.

When the permanent set is up it can be fixed to the stage floor (if allowed), and strengthened by fixing to walls or by the addition of battening or scaffolding. Then runs of flats are battened together, braces hinged on to them and the trucks are built. There is less chance of the fabric of cloths being damaged if they are flown or hung on the tab tracks after the solid structures have been built. Lights may then be rigged on the set if required – to light a doorway for the appearance of the Beast, perhaps, or to provide firelight in Cinderella's kitchen.

This is the moment to start working out where the component parts of the scenes are to be stored in the wings so that each scene is available to be moved as speedily as possible behind the front-cloths (or indeed, in full view, or in a blackout for transformations.) The interval may have to be spent moving all the scenes so they are in the correct places for Act Two. Space must be found to place prop tables so that actors may collect their props from the side of the stage through which they enter, and possibly to hang costumes and provide mirrors and lights for quick costume changes.

Consideration must be given to painting the floor, if this is required by the designer. If it is to be painted a solid colour, one coat can be applied before the fit up, which will be much easier on an empty stage, then a second one once the set is up. If the design is more complex, however, the scenic artist will have to wait till after the fit up, or the design will be damaged and it will probably be impossible to touch it up. It will need to be covered by a strong, non-slip glaze before any further work

Aladdin's 'jewels' are created in the workshop.

takes place on the stage, and must be finished before the lighting session, as the reflection from it will affect the appearance of the lit scenes.

BACKSTAGE AT THE PANTO

A pantomime performance seen from backstage always appears chaotic. Stage managers have the satisfaction of knowing that the chaos is completely hidden from the audience. The proof of this is the sense of wonderment that seeps onto the stage from the auditorium: the boos and cheers, the laughter, the singing, and the comments from young and old alike. It is stage management that pulls all the disparate elements together to make the show.

Ruth Staines studied Drama at Bristol University, working at the theatres of the Bristol Old Vic as well as on university productions. Shortly after this she worked for the Oxford Playhouse, before settling in Chipping Norton where she is Resident Stage Manager of The Theatre. For many years she has made props and built and painted the scenery for its celebrated annual pantomime.

8 PANTOMIME MAGIC
By Tina Bicât, Ruth Staines and Colin Winslow

Pantomime worlds are full of magic. It can hide behind every tree in the pantomime forest. The most wonderful and serene happenings onstage are usually the result of frenzied activity behind the scenes. The techniques that are described in this chapter work in situations where facilities are limited and ingenuity has to take the place of splendid equipment. If you have access to flies and traps, revolves and moving stage sections you will have no trouble in adapting these ideas for better-equipped spaces.

A GENERAL GUIDE TO PANTOMIME MAGIC

This section holds the very practical key to making magic work. Theatre magic relies on airy recipes, of which sound, light, music effects and diversionary tactics are the most common ingredients. And ingenuity. Perhaps most vital of all ingredients is the way the actor manages to combine the technical precision of his or her movements and handling of props with a belief in the magic. It is hard to understand that an actor can, in one moment, be stuffing plaster eggs into a prop chicken's neck with one hand, making the puppet react to some completely different event with the other hand, speaking his lines, moving into position under a specific light and still hold a belief in the character he is playing. But actors can and do, and unless they can and do, the audience won't believe in the magic. Pantomime magic calls for great concentration and long, repetitive work from actors and stage management to make it work.

DIVERSIONARY TACTICS

Much theatre magic relies, like a conjuring trick, on the audience's attention being diverted. Ingenuity and imagination, those good old free standbys, may have to replace technology. Whatever the means, the trick is to imagine how you would react as an innocent audience member caught up in the story. If you stand in a crowded place and stare with fixed and apparently fascinated attention at an imaginary object, or try to pick up a non-existent something that is apparently stuck to the floor, you can note the effect your interest has on other people. Leave the fascinating nothing behind the bench, the recalcitrant object on the floor, and you will see that others, according to their natures, peer or wander past with a sidelong glance to see what's up. Some, the less self-conscious ones, may bend down or get out their spectacles or scratch the empty floor. If you shout and point with enough energy

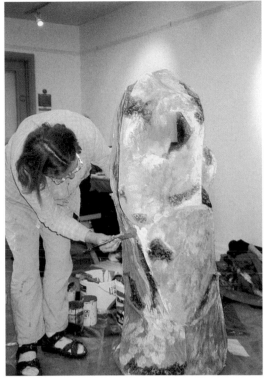

Newspaper, glue and paint make the magical dancing stones in a fairy-tale forest.

and conviction at an imaginary dromedary on a railway line, a whole platform full of people would turn to the direction of your pointed finger to see what made you react in such a way.

This instinctive reaction to a combination of sound and movement is the key to making the magic work. Using the two lures together is a way of hedging your bets; some people react more vigorously to sound and some to movement. The sound may draw some heads to turn away from the stage but the movement of the heads, even if it is only slight, will encourage others to look as well. The diversion will be more successful if the audience cannot take in the event from which they are being diverted and the diversion in one eyeful; even a small head-movement makes a difference. The duration of the diversion is vital. Children and adults, who are not used to going to the theatre, will turn immediately to see what is going. Others need time and a clear message that they are supposed to turn round and look.

Diversionary Sound

A mouse squeaks in the corner or galloping hooves clatter urgently on tarmac. All hearing people will turn their attention towards the sound. The speed of the reaction is dictated by our self-protecting response to the apparent danger it heralds. The eyes turn slowly for a sidelong glance at the mouse (unless their owner is of the scream-and-leap-on-the-table school). The clattering hooves will make us hurry to see what's going on; we are affected by their urgency. A great crack of thunder or the report of a gun causes most people to duck, close their eyes and hunch slightly. This valuable second may give the Genie time to appear from Aladdin's magic lamp.

Diverting the Audience's Attention

In this excerpt Old Mother Shipton has to vanish down the trap. She draws the audience's attention to the back of the audience with the help of everyone onstage pointing or staring towards the back of the theatre, and with door slammings and crashes (provided by the front of house staff) at the back entrances to the auditorium.

The Elves reluctantly start to pick mushrooms which they put in sacks.
OLD MOTHER SHIPTON: (*She turns back to the audience*) That Baron's getting above himself – his woodcutters messing up my forest. I've a good mind to send the Ghost Coach to him one dark night. Doesn't believe in witches indeed. (*Looks at the audience.*) I hope you believe in witches. You'd better. Well just in case anybody doesn't. Let's try a little experiment shall we? If you turn and look hard at the back of the theatre – really crane your necks and strain your eyes . . .

There is a flash and a bang. The Wychwood music goes frantic and OMS vanishes in a puff of smoke, leaving only a sulphurous smell and a noise like the fizzing and popping of a Roman candle. The Stones are back in place and the bags of mushrooms are leaning against them.

These diversionary tactics give the vital seconds onstage for the magic to take place.

Diversionary Light

Eyes react automatically to changes in light. The pupils of our eyes open when it is dim to let in as much light as possible and close when it is bright to protect themselves from too much brightness. This reaction is as useful to the inventor of magic as it is to our eyes. And often as necessary. A sudden bright light, and every healthy eye in the audience will need a moment to adjust. A flicker from bright to dark to bright to dark will baffle its powers to adjust and make everything look unreal. A blackout will seem densely black for the first moments as the eyes adjust to their new state. Eyes take longer to adjust to a blackout if the scene before has been bright. The tiny moments, when sight is sorting itself out, are the moments when the impossible can appear to come true. It is a very short moment and calls for precise timing; it is easier to get it right if you understand how it works.

Light draws attention. We look at the bright places before we peer into the shadows. Imagine a character alone onstage. A spotlight lights a point away from him with a bright light. There is music or a sound effect but nothing else – no movement. The audience will turn their attention away from the actor towards the light and expect the next thing of interest to happen in its beam.

Preparing and fitting the gels that colour theatre light.

Diversionary Acting

Pointing, or even simply looking in a direction with enough concentration, works onstage as in life and will cause the audience to look to see what's going on, and take attention away from the actor herself. Actors can draw the attention of the audience towards themselves, and away from anything or anyone else onstage, with a variety of simple tricks. For example, an actor takes a step forward, flourishes a handkerchief, scratches an insect bite, buttons her shoe and, providing other activity onstage is performed in a less energetic manner, the eyes of the crowd will follow her movements. Few things, apart from a young child or an animal onstage, will distract them. Children and animals have an unconscious ability to pull the interest of an entire and vast auditorium to themselves, whether wanted or not, just by being themselves. This naive talent is not always welcome, and should be taken into account when planning diversionary tactics.

ELEMENTAL EFFECTS

Fire

We can be convinced by an orange coloured light dressed with sticks and glowing in a grate. And more convinced if it flickers. A flame-effect gobo and a crackling sound effect can create an exciting blaze. Battery wands, candles and nightlights are available from specialist theatrical shops. Hand-held battery-powered lights, which are made for lighting spaces like cupboards, can be very useful on a small stage. Include the cost of batteries in the running budget of the show. There is also available a small wind machine that blows a flame-shaped scrap of silk over a fiery light, which is a safe and effective alternative to real flames.

Safety!

All pyrotechnic effects are inherently dangerous. Only use those designed for stage use and follow the manufacturer's instructions to the letter. Take stringent safety precautions: scenery and drapes must be fireproofed. 'Flambar' is usually recommended for stage work. Pyrotechnics must only be handled by a trained and responsible person, and must be stored under lock and key. Always check with your local fire officer, who will visit and offer advice. At no time must the health and safety of anyone – audience, cast and company – be put at risk, however splendid the effect. Flying, pyrotechnics and so on are dangerous activities and should only be performed by trained people who observe the relevant current rule book to the letter.

Smoke and Mist

There may be no smoke without fire in real life, but in pantomime it happens all the time. The magic pantomime characters appear and disappear in a puff of smoke for practical as well as magical reasons. Smoke, created by the smoke machine or smoke pellets, wafts its way into pantomime palaces, forests and dungeons. Mist swirls round the castle gate. A truly marvellous fast-flowing river of thick mist can be created with dry ice, but it is dangerous, expensive and difficult to store. It can burn and so must be handled with industrial gloves, and be stored in an airtight container. Apart from their magical ambiance, swirling clouds provide a practical screen to baffle the eyes of the audience and a convenient one that vanishes of its own accord when it is not wanted, unlike most other stage props. It is possible to colour mist with light – green for

A puff of smoke heralds the Genie.

the villain, pink for the good fairy, blue for the sea – and even to scent it with different perfumes. Beware that the theatre's smoke alarms may be affected by the mist and may have to be screened while the effect is in action.

Snow and Rain

Snow machines can be hired from specialist firms but it is more likely that the snowstorm will be a sprinkling of torn, flame-retardant paper: crêpe paper chopped into 1cm (½in) squares works well. Chop the paper into narrow strips and squares before you unfold it so that you can do lots at a time. These can be shaken from a perforated box in the flies if your theatre space has a fly tower. If not, the type of 'leaf drop' shown in the diagram can be used. The same system can be used for snow, confetti, glitter, feathers or anything else that must fall from above. It requires practice to release or pull the rope in such a way as to control the rate of sprinkle, so do not it expect it to work perfectly first time.

Rain can be projected onto the set from a hired rain projector. Sound effects, and umbrellas and mackintoshes sprayed with a plant spray, are a cheaper and simpler option. Make sure the stage light picks up the spray if it is a dark and stormy night on stage.

Wind

Wind machines can be hired or domestic fans can be used. Both make a noise, which may be all right in a storm but is not so good for magic. The effect required is to make costumes and parts of the set move as if receiving the force of the moving air. A sheet of polystyrene A3 size and about 3cm (1in) thick can be waved by an ASM off stage. Several ASMs and bigger sheets of polystyrene positioned in the best place can make quite an effective wind, provided there is something onstage that is light enough to react to it.

Flashes and Lightning

There are two main types of flashes. One of them, a pyrotechnic device available in various sizes, is a fierce and most effective

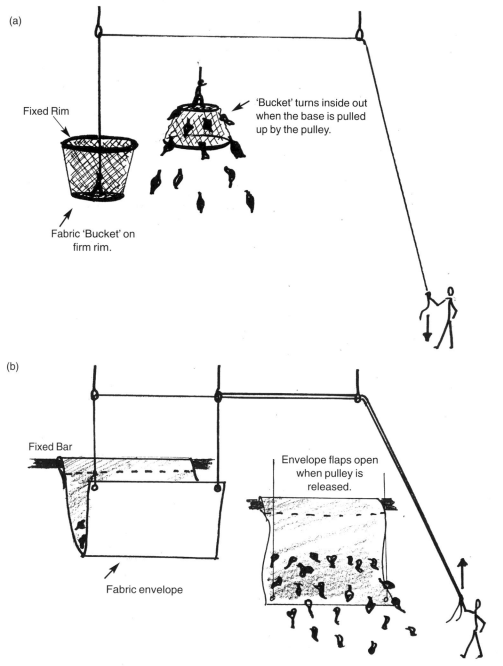

(a)

Fixed Rim

'Bucket' turns inside out when the base is pulled up by the pulley.

Fabric 'Bucket' on firm rim.

(b)

Fixed Bar

Envelope flaps open when pulley is released.

Fabric envelope

Two ways of working a leaf drop, or snow or glitter fall. It is easier to control the rate of sprinkle with (a) than with (b).

flash-and-bang. It has its disadvantages. There are guidelines relating to minimum distances between the device and any person or object onstage or in the auditorium. And, of course, it can only be used once, which may add considerably to the running budget of the show. The alternative type of flash is created by the stage lights flicking on and off, in which case it is the contrast between the two lighting states that creates the effect; a flash in a sunlit scene will not appear as bright as a flash in a moonlit one. Most lighting desks are equipped with a flash button; otherwise a series of mini blackouts spaced in clusters does the trick.

Bangs

A sound that is not particularly loud must be long and slow so that the audience have time to register and react to it: the sound of footsteps going upstairs, the splash of waves as the storm builds. A loud sound must be strong enough to cause an instant reaction in every person in every part of the auditorium. It can be a recorded sound, in which case the volume at which it will be introduced will be set in advance, or a live sound created by the stage management offstage, though it is hard to make that loud enough.

LIGHT

Blackouts

The screening properties of light are naturally the most powerful of all. A simple blackout is the most straightforward and surprisingly difficult to achieve. The emergency lighting required by the Health and Safety legislation lights up the exits from the auditorium and any changes of level. It is illegal to extinguish them, but if there are spare people around

they could hold up a small screen on a stick to baffle the light safely. The safety of the audience remains a priority at all times.

Musicians need the lights on their music stands: blue bulbs for the band, the prompt corner and the wings will lessen the glow; and the band could be asked to switch off their lights for the blackout. Blackouts are most effective for the first few seconds; the shorter they can be, the better.

Tips for Blackouts

It is usual for the operator to call out 'Going to black!' as a warning before a blackout during technical work onstage. If you have to perform a task (such as helping with a quick change) during a blackout, shut your eyes for a minute just before the lights are snapped off. This means your pupils will have had time to adjust and you will be able to see more in the dark than you could otherwise. There is a general safety rule in the theatre that if a blackout occurs unexpectedly everyone should keep absolutely still and await instructions from the stage manager.

Strobe

Strobe lighting, a light which flashes on and off, creates a jerky effect rather like a silent film. It baffles the eye with its flickering and can cover the movements of scenery and actors even when they are in view. The rate of flicker is adjustable. It is mandatory to warn the audience if strobe lighting is going to be used as it can have a severe effect on anyone suffering from epilepsy.

Gobos

There are wonderful effects that make water ripple, flames flicker and clouds fly. If you have money in the budget, space in your theatre and a skilled designer to play with lighting effects, you can make the whole world on your stage with light. For those without these resources there are gobos that work like light stencils and can create beautiful and magical effects. They are punched with a pattern and fitted in the slots provided in a profile lantern. The pattern appears where the light falls. You can create a stained-glass window, the pattern of leaves on the forest floor and the waves on the sea.

Mirror Ball

The mirror ball, which is available in various sizes, transforms every surface touched by its light. It is, perhaps, the most magical screen of all. Those who have not seen it before will greet its use with breath-held amazement and those who know its effect will still be delighted by its enchantment. It is the paradigm of theatrical wizardry – a simple little ball of mirrors that turns and reflects the light from its surface of tiny mirrors, and in doing so flies the audience to another world. Lights must be focused on it from appropriate directions to create a starry sky or fill the auditorium with glorious flying stars.

USEFUL ILLUSIONS

The Traveller-Cloth

This is, in effect, a curtain that is several times the width of the stage and painted with the background of a journey. We might see Dick Whittington, on his way to London, passing through country villages and the streets of London (not, alas, paved with gold!) and ending at Alderman Fitzwarren's front door. The actor makes his journey by walking on the spot; the cloth rolls the countryside past behind him. The curtain can be on a straight track that extends into the wings on either side. If your traveller-cloth is not very high, it could be drawn across by hand from behind with the aid of rods attached to the runners. A higher, heavier cloth may need three stage management members to move it: one helping it onstage from the wings on one side, one helping it off in the wings on the other side, and a third, in the middle, helping it across by means of vertical flaps of cloth glued onto the back of the canvas that distribute the strain and keep the cloth taut. Allow plenty of time to rehearse this.

The Vision

Pantomime plots often need the help of mystical visions. The prince is spurred on through the thorny forest by a vision of his Sleeping Beauty. The Beast's Beauty sees her dear, dying father in another. So many of these magical mirages spur the inhabitants of Pantoland into action. Most of them work on the principle that we can see light passing through a thin fabric but our eye is baffled by light bouncing off it. Try it. Hold anything made of thinnish fabric over a dark background. It is opaque. Hold it up to the day-lit window or the light bulb and you can see through it. Onstage these 'transformation gauzes' look best if they are incorporated into some sort of frame – it could be painted panelling on the wall, a picture frame, a gap framed by the branches of a tree or whatever is appropriate to the setting. When the vision is to be seen, the light on it must be behind the gauze, and when it should be invisible the gauze should be lit from the front. The gauze ('sharkstooth' for best effect)

A front-cloth allows the stage management to work behind it while the actors perform in front.
Photo: Rod Staines

can be painted to blend in with the rest of the scenery.

Mirrors Onstage, Magic or Otherwise

Real mirrors can seldom be used onstage as they tend to reflect things the audience shouldn't see. Make sure, if you do use them, that you check their reflection from every part of the auditorium. A great deal goes on backstage in pantomime that would destroy any audience's illusion if they could see the activity. Real mirrors should be sprayed or soaped to make them less reflective, as the stage light reflected into the audience's eyes can be dazzling. The Wicked Queen's mirror-on-the-wall tells the unwelcome truth through its magic surface. There is a plastic mirror sheeting that works like gauze and can be used when a reflection has to come to life. When lit from the front it is a looking glass; when the scene behind it is lit, the 'glass' becomes transparent.

The Revelation

A magic revelation can be produced by a sliding, flying or dropping panel that replicates exactly the scenery behind it. There is a space wide enough to contain an actor between the two. When the magic moment comes – Flash! Bang! The panel is slid, flown or dropped out of sight and the Genie, fairy, villain or other magic character appears. It will work best if there is some sort of natural colour change, such as a doorway or a gap between two trees, to disguise the edges of the panel. It should be upstage rather than downstage and lit to produce no shadow on the scenery behind.

Swimming on Stage

Puss-in-Boots tricks his young master into swimming. The river surface can be hidden from the audience by a ground-row of 'reeds', and the actor can 'swim' by lying on a small, wheeled platform pulled across the stage by a member of stage management in the wings.

The magic mirror hangs in its golden frame. Photo: Rod Staines

Another rope can be payed out from the wings on the other side to keep the swimmer on the right track if things start to veer off course. The same method can propel a swan, a magic carpet or anything that must float or glide. It may be necessary to lay a strip of carpet so that the wheels don't make a noise.

Falling Trees

A tree (or beanstalk) must be felled by the woodcutter's axe. The sound effects that accompany the action compensate for the fact that logistics in the less well-equipped company prevent the tree crashing through the air at the speed decreed by gravity: the chopping of the axe, the creaking of the straining wood and the mighty crash followed by the sound of settling branches are as important as the visual picture. The tree can be pivoted in the wings like a giant lever and can be controlled by a fishing line through a pulley above the place where it stands.

Giants

Fourteen-foot high animatronic giants must be left to productions with gigantic budgets. For smaller-scale productions, giants may be heard but not seen, or only partially seen – perhaps an enormous boot, or a hand. A tall actor, wearing built-up boots and a padded costume, could appear on a set with overlarge furniture that makes the other actors look small. Stilts, of course, will add to the actor's height. They vary enormously from the simple peg stilts of childhood to the slightly sprung plasterers' stilts, which adjust in height and allow a more normal gait, to a splendid invention, sprung with a half hoop of metal, on which the wearer can leap, dance and somersault. A more complex giant could use a full head mask worn by one actor sitting on another's shoulders, their duality covered by a full-length cloak. A three-headed ogre could have three masked heads on three actors in one costume. Eyes can light up, with bulbs powered by batteries, or the eyeballs roll if

Putting the finishing touches to the giant's head. Photo: Mike Cockburn

made of ping-pong balls on simple wire pivots, their attached controlling strings threaded through small screw eyes. The mouth or hairpiece can be made to move in much the same way.

TRICK PROPS

Eccentric Machinery

Some scripts may call for ridiculous machines such as Widow Twankey's washing machine that shrinks clothes, or the plate-smashing dishwasher in Cinderella's kitchen. The machine should be recognizable for what it is – the washing machine will be a white box with a circular window – but the more belts, pulleys, flashing lights and sound effects, the better. Silly noises can play when it starts up, a bubble machine can be built in, red lights can flash, smoke can start pouring out and finally it can explode with a small battery-operated pyrotechnic.

The Patent Wobbly Washing-up Machine. Photo: Rod Staines

The Magic Table

A splendid banquet is set out on a table – golden bowls of glowing fruit and plates of gorgeously decorated cakes and jewel-like jellies. A flash and a crash, and the table is suddenly a mess of rotting food overrun with rats! The table top is, of course, on a spindle with the delicious food glued onto one side and the revolting mess on the other. A cloth hangs down and conceals the underside of the table.

The Cage of the Hen that Lays the Golden Egg

The hen is in her cage in the Giant's castle. A tube runs from the bottom of the cage to a hole in the scenery representing the wall behind the cage. As the bird clucks as if laying, an egg is put into the tube by an ASM offstage and rolls down to the floor of the cage and into the audience's view. A stick poking through another small hole in the flat into a socket in the back of the bird will enable the hen to be animated.

Robin Hood's Target

The arrow is shot from the bow and quivers in the centre of the target. The actor actually palms the arrow to his upstage side while, on the target, a spring-loaded arrow hinged on the bull's-eye is released by a member of the stage crew concealed behind the target stand.

The arrow that is to be split by Robin Hood will have handles like scissors at the back of the target. These can be manipulated by a Stage Manager, to split away an outer arrow leaving an inner one sticking out of the target.

Cobwebs

Cans and spray guns that create cobwebs on the set can be bought from specialist suppliers. Grey muslin or cotton netting shredded and festooned over the Sleeping Beauty's bed create a good effect and can be decorated with the occasional sequin, a dab of glitter or a predatory spider.

Walking the Plank

The plank must be fixed firmly on a well-made bit of set. The actor must walk so that he lands upstage or offstage. Something, the side of the boat or a ground row of waves, conceals his body as he falls and the splashing and yells leads the audience to imagine the rest.

PANTOMIME SPECIALS

Here are some ways to amaze the audience. They use more ingenuity than expensive equipment, and solve some of the pantomime problems that surface every Christmas.

The table before and after the rats.

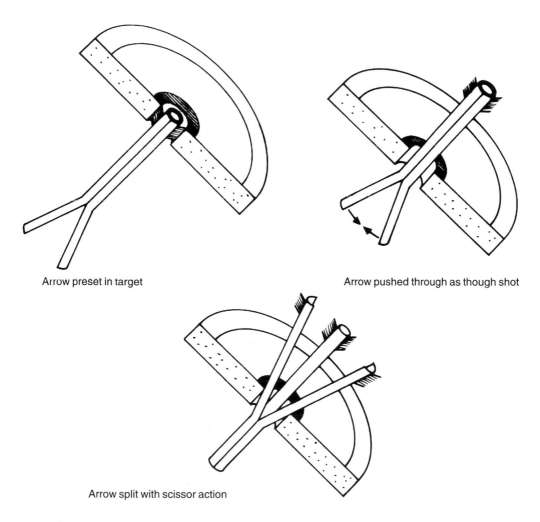

Arrow preset in target

Arrow pushed through as though shot

Arrow split with scissor action

How Robin Hood splits the arrow.

Growing the Beanstalk

Theatres equipped with a fly-floor and traps, with space above and below the visible stage area, will have no problems. Those with neither, or with limited height and depth, must be more ingenious. Paint the beanstalk on a long sheet of scene canvas, cutting away any unpainted areas and, if necessary, gluing scenic net on the back for extra support. Horizontal battens may be required to keep the canvas from curling at the edges. The whole sheet can then be wrapped around a roller, which is a bit wider than the beanstalk and supported at each end so that it can unroll freely when the top of the beanstalk is drawn up to maximum height by means of heavy-gauge nylon fishing line attached to the top. The whole thing can be hidden behind a painted flower bed or garden wall. This means that the beanstalk could be very wide at the

129

Fly-and-Truck

Excellent effects can be produced by a combination of a cut border hanging from above and a lower section being pushed or hauled on as a truck. The trunk of a tree and its leaves, for instance or the balloon and its basket.

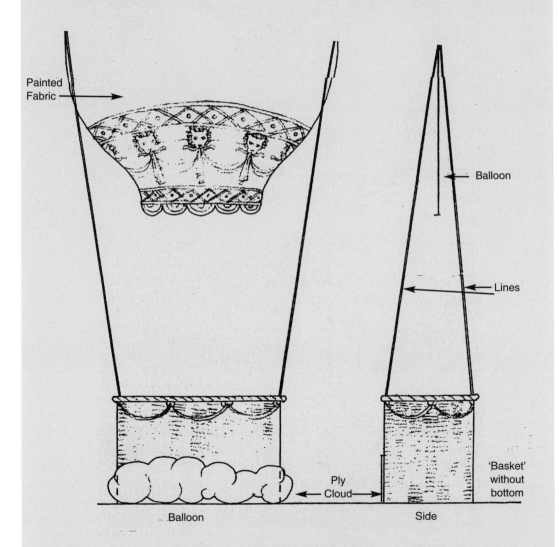

Painted Fabric

Balloon

Lines

'Basket' without bottom

Ply Cloud

Balloon

Side

A balloon on a cloth on a track; the basket is on a wheeled truck propelled by actor inside it.

Fly-and-Truck *continued*

A balloon on a track and a basket on invisible wheels.
Photo: Rod Staines

The hollow tree-trunk is a truck, the foliage a painted cloth.
Photo: Rod Staines

bottom, and really fill the stage when fully grown. If a trapdoor is available, then the beanstalk can grow up through the stage in a similar manner.

Jack cannot, of course, climb a beanstalk made of a sheet of painted canvas hanging on a nylon thread. However, as soon as the beanstalk is fully grown, a narrow ladder can be lowered in immediately behind it. Make sure the beanstalk is wide enough to hide it. The bottom of the ladder needs to be firmly fixed, by being pegged into a specially prepared frame under the stage or hidden in the 'flower bed'. Once the ladder is secured, Jack can begin his climb, visible through the cut-away areas of the beanstalk, and, of course, leaning out as far as possible to wave goodbye.

Don't be tempted to use a rope ladder – it will swing about in a very alarming way, and is far more difficult to climb than you may imagine – especially if you are a traditional Principal Boy in high heels and fishnets.

Cinderella Goes to the Ball

Not only does the pumpkin transform into a coach, but the whole kitchen vanishes as Cinderella sets off for the ball. A kitchen scene can be designed with a pair of very wide doors in the rear wall. This means that the back wall can actually be constructed on a pair of trucks, each with a door hinged to the leading edge. When the pumpkin is placed outside, the doors are opened right back against the walls. The painted scene we see through the open doors is actually a small backcloth – just wide enough to mask the doorway. Behind this cloth is a duplicate full-size cloth set a couple of metres behind the first one. Between these two painted cloths, Cinderella's coach is set with one or more well-mannered white ponies. Cinderella places the pumpkin on a strip of scene canvas painted the same colour as the stage floor, so that when the Fairy Godmother casts her spell, under cover of a pyrotechnic flash and cloud of magic smoke, the pumpkin is pulled off; the small backcloth is flown out to reveal the coach; the rear-wall trucks are drawn off to right and left, and the kitchen wings (on periaktoi) revolve to show snow-covered trees.

'Cinderella, you shall go to the ball!' says the Fairy Godmother, a wand is waved and the ragged girl appears in her ball gown, the

The beanstalk grows from the cottage garden to the Giant's castle in the clouds.
Photos: Rod Staines

pumpkin turns to a coach and the rats to splendid footmen. How?

The Fairy Godmother has a very big cloak; perhaps a whole circle or more which comes down to her feet. Cinderella, in her rags, has a double, also in the same rags. Cinderella is sent outside by Godmother to get the pumpkin. She puts on her threadbare, hooded cloak, goes off-stage and begins her frantically quick change into ball gown, jewels, dancing shoes and the rest. The double, an identical threadbare hood up to screen her face and facing slightly upstage, puts the pumpkin upstage centre and moves downstage to tend the fire or sweep a bit or some other suitable action that takes her nearer the wings. The wand is waved, the lights flash, the cloak swirls (covering, in the process, the exit of Cinderella's double and the entrance of the real Cinderella) and Cinderella is revealed, glittering and beautiful in her magical dress. It works because the audience knows, having seen Cinderella tending the fire a moment before, that she cannot have changed her costume in the time.

Ugly to Beautiful

This can be used when an actor wears a head mask as the Beast, an animal or a witch and must transform, in the blink of a flash, into a beautiful human.

The audience must be used to seeing the character in a mask; ideally, they will have seen him wearing a large cloak on some occasion. Offstage the actor changes his frog/witch/beast costume for the gorgeous outfit, but puts the cloak the audience has already seen over the top to hide his changed clothes. He has a replica mask which, instead of being a full head mask, is on a stick that he holds close to his face. He disguises the stick-holding hand in the fold of his cloak. When

the moment comes he can turn, drop the mask and cloak in a second (making sure the mask is concealed in the cloak) and reveal his hidden beauty! The cloak can also be a replica, cut more generously than the real one, and perhaps slit at the back rather than the front. The audience will not register the change as long as the colour and decoration of the cloaks is distinctive and they appear to be identical.

The Beast to the Handsome Prince

Beauty kisses the dying Beast, smoke and sound effects, music and light, and he changes into young love's dream. How?

He can either do it quickly in a flash of lightning and a blackout, in which case a double must be used. The beast must stagger upstage, groaning in his last throes. Beauty diverts the audience's attention to the other side of the stage by calling for help, ringing for servants

The beast's mask.

133

or some other diversion. The whole object of this is to allow the Beast, as far up-stage (i.e. as far away from the audience) as possible, to slip offstage and the double, looking exactly like him, to come on. The Beast groans his dying gasps (he does not speak, as that would give away the fact it is a different actor) and, after the shortest amount of dialogue or business that will allow for an actor offstage to change into his splendid costume, is kissed by Beauty. A flash, a blackout, a sound effect, and the Prince appears, having, of course, changed places with the double.

Alternatively, he can do it slowly, which involves the use of a more complicated costume change but no double. The beast has the prince's costume underneath his Beast costume. He may have to change shoes and mask for simpler versions just for this scene and must play the scene facing front as his costume must be opened down the back. He lies down and breathes his dying gasps between the pillars of an upstage gateway or doorway. There is a member of the stage management team, or a dresser, behind each pillar. There is rising smoke and a lighting effect. The dressers hold each end of his costume stretched tightly between them, so that he can rise up out of the split seam at the back, resplendent and princely while the costume is whisked out of sight behind the pillars.

The Genie of the Magic Lamp

The Genie and other characters that appear by magic traditionally appeared through a wonderful device called a star trap which shot the brave actor, poised under the stage, into the air through a trapdoor and deposited him on the stage. If the equipment and space is available he could drop out of the sky. Otherwise he must either appear from the wings or be revealed by trickery. In either case a blackout and, budget and space permitting, a flash effect and smoke must hide the vital moment from the audience.

An appearance from the wings means that Aladdin must rub the lamp close to the place where the Genie will appear. It must be timed perfectly, usually with a count from a particular gesture or a word that can be seen and heard by everyone involved. Blackout, flash and the Genie's jump must coincide exactly. Aladdin's astonishment, a sound effect and music and perhaps a special Genie light will reinforce the magic, and of course, good old smoke creates a mystical atmosphere with ever-fresh power.

The Hen that Lays the Golden Eggs

Jack steals the hen that lays golden eggs from the Giant at the top of the beanstalk and brings it back to earth. He carries the bird in his arms down the beanstalk. When we see it laying its eggs we see both his arms holding the puppet hen. In fact one of these arms is false, its hand half buried in the 'feathers'. The actor's real hand is in the puppet's neck and head, making it move in a lively manner. He is able to palm 'golden' eggs from a pocket and insert them into a tube, the opening of which is concealed by 'feathers' at the chicken's neck. The egg rolls down the tube inside the puppet and is 'laid'.

The hen is convincing only if the actor handles it as if it were a living creature, which takes time and rehearsal in front of the mirror to become familiar with the picture the audience sees. If the head is moved according to the actor's speech rather than the hen's own reactions, the joke is spoilt.

Sinbad's Roc

Sinbad is plucked from the stage by a huge bird that flies off into the air. A simple-enough affair with a safety harness and a fly floor. But what if your theatre has no space above the stage for flying equipment? Or not the money and skill to create a gigantic bird for him to fly on? One answer is to show the audience only a part of the bird – perhaps his feet. Their talons, on ropes, can drop down from pulleys. The ropes are covered with cloth painted to resemble feathered legs, which will concertina into a small space when the talons are drawn up. Sinbad will cling onto a talon and be drawn up as high as space, safety and the muscles of the stage management allow, accompanied by suitably dramatic wing-flapping and wind-rushing sound effects. The blackout, or closing of the tabs, must come, of course, at the moment of optimum height, though the sound effects can continue to carry him off into the sky.

Getting a Good Gold

It can be difficult to make gold paint look like bright, gold metal. Some types of spray paint look particularly shiny, but only where the surface is completely smooth and non-absorbent. Gold powder paint works well but only where the spectator is in the correct relative position to the object to catch the reflection of the light on the metallic particles. Imitation gold leaf, known as Dutch Metal, gives a beautiful surface on small objects but does not wear very well, even when varnished, if it is subject to much handling. Paint in a base yellow, with brown shadows and near-white highlights, often looks more gold than gold, and it can always be enhanced with random sequins.

A similar method with the beak or the foot of the bird appearing from the wings, and the ropes and pulleys concealed by flats, would haul Sinbad up at the side of the stage. In either case, unless the system is counter-weighted, the haulers must weigh more than the actor being lifted and be strong enough to perform their task easily and to land the actor safely back on the stage during the blackout.

Sinbad's Island

That Sinbad's island turns out to be a whale creates another problem. In the design shown on page 137, the base of the island is hidden

Working with a puppet in front of the mirror.

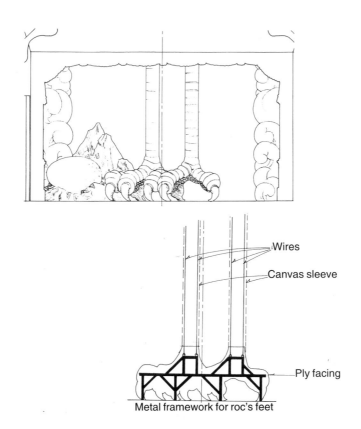

The roc descends.

Wires

Canvas sleeve

Ply facing

Metal framework for roc's feet

The roc's feet descend to carry off Sinbad. Photo: Rod Staines

by a 'sea-cloth' – a cloth stretched across the stage and made to wave by the ASMs who hold it in the wings. Pulleys raise the whale's head and tail, on the 'island', which then rise in the appropriate positions above the cloth and so the whale appears.

ACTORS AND MAGIC

The actors in the pantomime cast are the apparent creators and receivers of the magical effects created by the crew. They keep going, telling the story, singing the songs, dancing the dances through all the bangs, flashes and

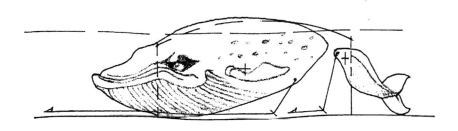

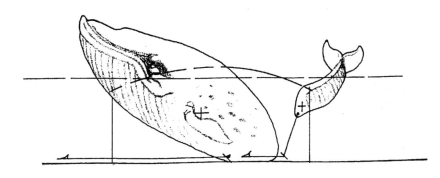

WHALE TRUCK

How the island becomes a whale. Photos: Rod Staines

smoke. They have to work with no idea, or at best an incomplete idea, of the picture and sounds the audience are receiving. They are the ones who are going to have to cope if the magic fails. It is most important that the trust they are obliged to place in the stage management, lighting and sound departments is well placed. An actor left onstage in a moment of vital change during a blackout has nothing and no-one to help if the blackout fails to materialize. Mistakes happen. But if they happen too often mutual trust and confidence between actor and crew ebbs away, and the vigour and sparkle of the production, which relies so much on the confident energy of the cast, ebbs away with it. Magic is only ever as good as the actors who perform with it; they are the ones who make the audience believe the impossible.

9 THE CHILDREN OF THE COMPANY

Most pantomime companies include a group of children. These can be trained professionals from a stage school with their own agents and governed by the strict licensing laws that limit and control the work of children in the theatre; or raw talent from the town who have never been on a stage before; or anything in between. Amateur or professional, they are still children, and extra care must be taken in the exciting environment of a theatre to make sure they are safe. The vitality, freshness and vigour they bring to the company should be recognized as a huge advantage, as should their commercial value as an audience draw. Their energy and lively interest can prove a bit of a burden to the less-experienced or nervous members of the cast. The children of the company should always have a space of their own, which will usually double as their dressing room, where they can let off steam in the care of their chaperone.

Even where the law does not require the children to have an official chaperone it is better for everyone if one group of adults has particular responsibility for the children in the theatre. It is easy to lose track of the whereabouts of a child when there is no definite system in place. Or to discover, after questioning listless behaviour in the afternoon, that the

Most young children, amateur or professional, love dressing up and performing.
Photo: Chris Smith

child didn't know she was supposed to bring a packed lunch and so has had nothing to eat since breakfast. The schedule of the day

140

should be made clear to parents and guardians as well as to the children. A packed lunch is often a better option than trying to keep tabs on which children are allowed to shop in the town by themselves and which are only allowed out with an adult.

Professional Children

Professional children with stage school training will be used to the discipline of the rehearsal and dressing room. Their dancing and singing training will mean they can learn the routines and songs of the pantomime quickly. Their performances will usually be more polished than those of the amateur child and their adult approach to the work and familiarity with the theatrical environment and its rules and routines can make people for-

get that, under their professional veneer, they are still children, and need to have fun and be looked after at all times.

Amateur Children in a Professional Company

These young people are often drawn from a Youth Theatre connected to a theatre, a local school or dance class. They have been chosen from many other young hopefuls and are usually delighted and excited by their success. It should be made clear to both them and their parents that their inclusion in the company carries certain conditions and that there will be a lot of hard work as well as fun. It is a commitment for the parents as well as the children. Their parents will have to arrange for their delivery and collection from the theatre both throughout rehearsals and performance.

PARENTAL CONSENT FORM

Name of child: _____

Home Address: _____

_____ Postcode: _____

Contact Tel Nos: _____ Mobile: _____

School: _____

Address: _____
(including Postcode)

Family Doctor & Surgery Address: _____

Known Medical Conditions: _____

Medicines	Category of Child			Dose	Method of Administration	When to be given (include time of day if appropriate)
	1. Able to self administer	2. Able to self administer under supervision	3. Needs medicine to be administered for them			

I give my permission for a Chaperone or nominee to administer or oversee administration of the above medicine to my son/daughter.

Signed: _____ (Parent/guardian/person with parental responsibility)

Date: _____

It is best If all parents sign a form that sets out the expectations clearly and provides a record of emergency numbers, special health or dietary problems, and so on.

Family holidays cannot be taken during the run of the show. Arrangements have to be made with schools for any time missed and schoolwork will have to be fitted into what becomes a very busy schedule. For their own safety as much as anything else they will all need to be taught the rules of the theatre.

Sensible Behaviour

It should be made clear at the beginning of rehearsals that both adults' and children's dressing rooms are private places. Problems are most likely to arise when the children fail to understand when actors need concentration and quiet, or even exclusively adult conversation, and the adults are unwilling to appear unfriendly with the children. Some children can manage to concentrate in the midst of a raging party; most adults cannot.

A teenager with a crush on an actor can make determined and embarrassing efforts to catch the attention of the object of affection. A clear guide to reasonable behaviour on both sides from the start of rehearsals will prevent irritated or worried complaints to the management from actors or parents. The chaperone should always know where the children are and children should always be supervised. Actors should remember that playful and innocent romping with children can be misconstrued, and keep a reasonable, but not snooty, distance. Children should be reminded to respect actors' privacy. If there is the slightest suspicion of a problem, the management should be alerted.

Despite the rather forbidding nature of this section, it is a fact that most adults in the theatre behave in the same straightforward and easy manner with children as they do with anyone else, enjoy working with them and make an effort to pitch their language and

behaviour suitably in front of their young colleagues. And the children of the company have a wonderful experience.

THE CHAPERONE

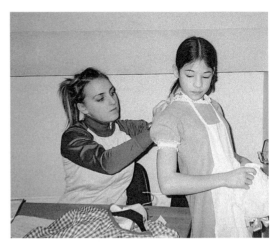

The chaperone helps a young actor with tricky costume fastenings.

Chaperones are responsible for the safety and welfare of the children in their care and the law requires them to have a licence and the appropriate police checks that permit them to do the job. The current details may vary slightly in different areas and information can be obtained from the local authority. This will set out the legal extent of their duties. But many chaperones do far more than the minimum requirement.

A good chaperone will control the children without staunching their exuberance. She will suggest games that interest but do not produce too much excitement; will make sure the children are where they should be when they should be and dressed in the right costume; will have the entrances, exits and costume changes and props under her belt; will spot early signs of fatigue, worry or illness; and will make sure the children keep their strength as a group and do not fragment into factions. She will tactfully steer them away from any happening in the theatre that is unsuitable for their age, and keep a strict and kindly eye on any hero-worshipping or star-struck youngster. Chaperones will also help with line learning, hear the children's songs, sew on buttons, watch them rehearse their dances and encourage their confidence and concentration, and usually do very much more than is stated in their contract. Most importantly, they keep the children safe and happy.

HEALTH AND SAFETY

Avoiding Danger

A theatre is an exciting building and chockfull of hazards for the unwary. Health and Safety laws will apply in the theatre but, as always, it is the responsibility of everyone in the building to take reasonable care. Children will be more likely to take notice of a rule if they know the reason why and the potential dangers are explained. You can tell a child that it is against the rules to stand in a certain place in the wings: if you explain that scenery is being lowered and might bash people on the head, and demonstrate that the adult actors also obey the rules, your advice will be remembered and adhered to.

Fitness to Work

The chaperone stands in place of the parent when the child is in the theatre. Children cannot always explain, and do not always say when they do not feel well. The chaperone will ring the child's parents if she considers that a child is ill or overtired, and inform the management so that a stand-in can be arranged for the performance. No medication should be

The Dame explains to interested children the reason for a delay at the tech.

given to a child without written instructions from their parent or guardian. Some companies require a daily show report to be filled in with any unusual happening during the course of the show.

Behaviour

The management will inform the parents officially of the rules and schedules for the young people in the company. It is a good idea for the chaperone to give a talk to her charges (and perhaps the parents as well) at the beginning of the rehearsals about the children's time backstage. Professional children will be familiar with the environment, but for others, theatre practice must be explained. It is no good expecting a child who has never hung up his clothes or listened out for his cue on the tannoy (a device that relays the sounds from the stage to the dressing rooms) to do so automatically. Children need to know what is expected of them, to be told that they are not allowed to wander alone round the theatre, that they must use the lavatories reserved for them, must never leave the building unless collected, and so on. It is equally important, amid all these rules and regulations, that the children have an exciting and rewarding experience and that despite all the hard work, they will have fun being part of the pantomime company.

Children understand very quickly that the professional actors in the company keep quiet when waiting in rehearsals, write down and remember any notes from the director, practise their dances and songs at odd moments and do not chuck their costumes on the floor or play with the props. With a bit of encouragement from the chaperone, they will do the same.

The chaperone will tell the management if a child's behaviour causes serious concern. The management will warn the parents and, if trouble persists, suspend the child from some performances. It is rare, however for a warning not to do the trick. Children know from the auditions how many there are who would love to be in their shoes and nearly all of them are there because they love dressing up and performing, and are happy to have the opportunity.

Fittings

Where there are costume changes, and there usually are in pantomime, it is helpful if the chaperone attends the fitting even if the parent is there too. A chaperone who knows what the young actors will wear, and when they will wear it, may rehearse the changes with her charges in the dressing room. Children cannot be hurried through a quick change, but they will speed up with practice. Experience will help the chaperone suggest ways of underdressing costumes (it is much quicker to take off a pair of tights revealing another underneath, than to put on a pair). Quick changes, though rehearsed at the tech, are not run within the timing of the show until the dress rehearsal. Children can become very worried and uncertain if they are not sure what to put on when, which will result in them slowing down a change or even stopping to ask questions. The chaperone, if she has not been in the position to prevent this happening, can at least make sure that no-one displays anger or

A boy experiments with the tail he will wear as a woodland animal.

Young actors arrange their costumes in order for their quick changes.

irritation that will destroy the children's confidence. She will always support and protect the interests of the child.

Food and Drink

Where there is no provision for meals within the theatre, children will be expected to bring their own packed meal to eat between the shows or on all-day rehearsal sessions, as well as snacks for other times. Children get thirsty and it is most important that they have access to drinking water if their own supplies run out.

Passing the Time

Child companies, professional or amateur, will be composed of children of different ages and experience. There can be a lot of sitting about in the dressing room, particularly on tech days. More experienced children can be encouraged to help out the younger ones with dance routines and to organize an unofficial rehearsal in the dressing room. Children will bring in board games, cards and puzzles, crafts and other relatively quiet time-passers. Anything like television or games that engross the child into not hearing the tannoy and listening for their cues, or rev everyone up to a pitch of uncontrollable excitement, should be discouraged. A quiet environment must be created for children who have homework to do.

Housekeeping!

Chaperones will encourage the children to clear up their games and toys, hang up their costumes and keep mess to a minimum. They collect costumes for washing and cleaning, allot the clean clothes and do small mending tasks. Their job, however, is to look after the children and not to wash and mend. In informal and amateur companies, parents will chip in and help, though there is always a possibility of costumes going astray if they are allowed out of the theatre. The best solution, when washing becomes problematic, is to make sure the children wear a T-shirt and socks of their own under their costumes so that these get washed at home and the actual costume does not leave the building.

All this may sound as if the chaperone has the mission statement of a guardian angel and this is, pretty well, what a good chaperone is. The advantage to the company of knowing the

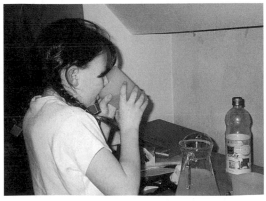

A thirsty moment off stage.

Children play in the dressing room while waiting for the 'beginners on stage' call.

children will be waiting quietly in the wings for their cues correctly dressed in the right costume for the scene and under a competent and watchful eye is inestimable. Chaperones bear a huge responsibility for the children in their charge in a challenging environment. They must insist on good behaviour but be loved and trusted as a friend. A good one, like a good teacher, is worth triple her weight in gold. She will be remembered, as the children she has looked after grow up, as an essential part of their unforgettable experience as a pantomime child, and in many cases will be responsible for ensuring that it is a happy one.

CHILDREN IN REHEARSAL

The discipline of the rehearsal room can come as a surprise to some children. And to their parents. The times when they have nothing to do but sit quietly watching others work is for them more arduous and requires more self-control than learning the most energetic dance. However their presence in the rehearsal room can become invaluable as an audience: they will provide the hisses and boos and comment of audience participation that will give the actors a foretaste of what's to come when they perform in front of a real audience.

Concentration
One of the greatest challenges when rehearsing children is ensuring their concentration onstage when they have no lines or action of their own. They need to learn the importance of listening and looking at the action onstage, not at the audience or at anything else that catches their attention. Most pantomime companies work with two teams of children. Each child has a partner of the same height in the opposite team, and when one group is onstage rehearsing, the other is watching, learning the moves and writing notes in their scripts. Theatrically trained children learn dance routines and moves quickly, but for newcomers there is a huge amount of information to be absorbed after a tiring day at school. The

Young performers study their scripts during a pause in rehearsal.

goodwill and friendliness of the company, along with a professional attitude to the work, makes a great difference to the enjoyment, confidence and performance of the children.

Directing Children

A few children appear to be born actors and work in the same way as the adults in the company. Most children do not have an instinctive grasp of the space they take up onstage or the way they appear as a group to the audience. They need clear, uncomplicated instructions and to know exactly what they are supposed to be doing and what they are supposed to be feeling like. An uncertain or ill-at-ease child onstage will look acutely uncomfortable, and the audience will feel uncomfortable with him. A child who is confident, certain and enjoying himself will create for the audience some of the most enjoyable moments in the pantomime. Notes from the director, musical director and choreographer must be easy to understand: the chaperone can help by going over the notes with the children in the dressing room and making sure all ages have taken them on board.

A simply choreographed dance performed with happy confidence will create a much better effect than a complicated one with worried children bumping into each other and frowning in concentration. There is a big gulf between acting-school training, which teaches children to dance as a puppet-like section of a group, and the ordinary schoolchild who is given choreographed dance for the first time. Audiences love to see children. The children enjoy performing. Everyone gets the best deal if the work the children are expected to do is within their capabilities.

Understudies

Children are prone to illness in the winter months and there will invariably be performances when a child is not well enough to go on stage. There may be an understudy for each team who has rehearsed the children's roles along with the rest of the team and can step in. It is hard for a child to understudy, particularly in the technical and dress rehearsals as they must spend so much time sitting quietly and watching. If possible, it should be arranged that they should appear in some performances, whether anyone is ill or not. Where there is no understudy a member of the other team will be asked to step in.

Prop Fiddling

The props tables act like a magnet to children in the wings. It should be explained that nothing on the stage must be touched or moved unless it is part of their performance. Demonstrate that props are all checked in the correct position before each show and that difficulties might ensue onstage if a prop was missing or not available for easy grabbing by an actor rushing onstage. Be warned that any weapon in the wings will exert an almost irresistible fascination to boys.

Director and choreographer give notes to the children after rehearsal.

Children in school uniform rehearse their dance.

CHILDREN IN PERFORMANCE

As the run progresses and life in the theatre settles to a regular routine, it is easy for children to become blasé and a bit bored with performing. The excitement and novelty dies away and the performance can feel, to some children, like just another way of using up their holiday time. Children have a strong sense of fairness and need only a reminder that a lack of concentration on their part affects all the other performers. A sympathetic chaperone will notice any lapses, chat to the child unofficially and keep things up to scratch.

It might seem a tough way for a child to spend their Christmas holiday. Hard work. Rigid discipline. Hot and tiring. Repetitive. But ask a child who has been in a pantomime company and most, whether professional, amateur or anywhere in between will tell you that they have had a wonderful time. They remember all their lives the fun, the games and jokes. They love being part of a team, dressing up, and the camaraderie of the company backstage. Pantomimes need children backstage as much as they need them in the audience to radiate their irreplaceable and indefinable energy and excitement.

Two little fairies compare wands.
Photo: Anna Turk

10 Curtain Up

A feeling of panic begins to rise within the company as the first night approaches. Everyone longs for more time. Worries and tensions rise as the tiredness engendered by the hard days of preparation begins to be felt. In every department of the theatre there is an increase in speed and urgency: sewing machines in the wardrobe, power tools in the workshop, glue brushes in the prop room, and singing and line-muttering everywhere. The first and most arduous herald of the first night is the technical rehearsal.

The Technical Rehearsal

A pantomime technical rehearsal is a test of endurance, concentration and self-control. It may be the first time that the actors have seen and worked on the set. It will be the first time the music, scenery, lighting, sound, costume changes, entrances and exits, which work so fluently in rehearsal, are worked in real time with real objects. Songs sound different in the empty auditorium and there may be the complication of mikes to cope with. Costumes that seemed comfortable in the wardrobe prove difficult to dance in, and their entrances and exits are obstructed by the pieces of set stored in the wings. Sitting and waiting is the worst part of any tech. The list of jobs to be done in every department gets longer and longer.

Every technical cue, exit and entrance must be tested and rehearsed. It is not an acting rehearsal. It is an opportunity for actors who have been working with stand-in props and furniture to use the real objects in the actual space, wearing the clothes they will wear in performance. They may not have rehearsed at all in the theatre space and will certainly be unfamiliar with many aspects both of the set and of the backstage space. Entrances and exits that have become familiar as marks on the rehearsal room floor will look unfamiliar now they have become doors, windows and openings in a painted, three-dimensional environment.

There will be long pauses, when a problem in one department causes everything to grind to a halt. This may give the wardrobe an opportunity to alter a button, the choreographer time to suggest a different entrance for his group of elves where they can skip onstage more quickly, the MD to work out incidental music for a scene change or for the ASM to discuss with the Giant a convenient place in the wings to set down the axe. Everyone remains easily available as no-one knows how long a hold-up will last and how soon they will be needed again.

The special effects and transformations, most of which involve a mixture of stage management, lighting, costume and sound expertise, not to mention considerable dexterity and aplomb from actor and dancer, create holdups: the tech will be the first chance that all the departments have to see the result of the melding of their work and the attempt to blend them together is often disastrous. Lights and sound lose synchronization; set changes jam; costumes won't button or slip off or on in time; the music isn't long enough for the transformation; actors forget lines; it feels, too, as if some ideas, so wonderful at their conception, might fall apart at their birth.

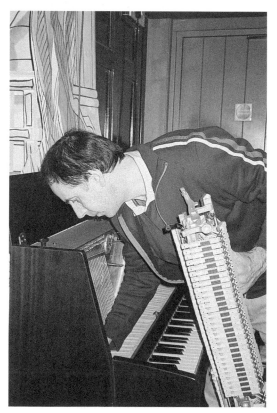

The piano gets an urgent repair before the dress rehearsal.

Choreographer

Dance routines seem crushed by the substantial scenery which was represented in the rehearsal room by markings on the floor and the odd chair. All the exits and entrances feel inconvenient to the performers now that there are three-dimensional objects to work round. Track suits and rehearsal clothes are replaced by unfamiliar costumes. The rescuing hero cannot swing onstage on a rope because the cut of his jacket stops his arms going higher than his shoulders and there's a whacking great truck with Daisy the Cow's byre on it blocking the entrance. Shoes slip, knickers show when they shouldn't, or don't show when they should, and the servants of the palace, who come onstage in a blackout, are in danger of falling into the orchestra pit. The children are bored with hanging around and the chaperone is having a tough time keeping them in order.

The choreographer will check that everyone can move safely. He will adjust the movements to fit in or fill the space, and make sure the dancers can get on and off the stage easily. His object, like everyone else's, is to make sure all the problems are smoothed away before the dress rehearsal.

The Musical Director

The composer and the MD will have been able to make an educated guess at how long are the scene changes and business that are accompanied by the band. The tech gives them the opportunity to judge if they were right. Set, costume and lighting changes take time to sort out, and the pauses give the MD and the band time to address any changes. There may be too much or too little music in a cue; if the band has several players, new variations may be written by the composer or the variations may be created from the pantomime score by the MD. It depends on the size of the band whether the new music is rehearsed at a band call, in a more informal manner during pauses in the tech, or at a session afterwards.

The Set Changes

There will be small adjustments needed to the painting of the set, which will become apparent when it can be seen in the stage light. The designer will check each scene from the auditorium and note anything that needs to be touched up or repainted. The set changes and transformations have to be rehearsed. There is often as much elaborate choreography going on with the huge pieces of set and props backstage as there is with the chorus of dancers in front of the curtain. Large flats need rehearsed and careful balancing, as well as strength, to be moved safely. Changes often take place while the actors are playing a front-cloth scene, so they must be performed quietly, and probably quickly; both scene change and front-cloth scene must be timed together.

The changes are the tip of the iceberg. Space in the wings is crowded and limited, and the stage crew rehearse a planned and silent juggling act throughout the play to ensure there is enough room for the actors in the wings, the correct flat or truck is at the front ready for the next change, exits are not blocked and the area is organized so that it is safe as well as practical.

The Stage Manager will have assessed the relative strengths of her team and everyone will know exactly what they will be moving in each scene change. Each crew member will have a list of their particular tasks and cue lines. The Stage Manager may have to enlist extra help from the actors, or make sure that they are out of harm's way for a quick set

change. The Stage Manager of a pantomime, unseen by the audience, plays a starring role.

The Props

The props are made, the lists complete and every item is set and checked on the prop tables in the wings and in the actors' dressing rooms. The exact position of each prop on the tables will be marked so that an actor knows where to find it. Personal props, such as fans and handkerchiefs, will be kept in the dressing rooms and checked by stage management before each show. Actors who have been rehearsing with stand-in props will be learning what the real thing feels like; their unfamiliarity with the weight and size may cause difficulties and questions. Many of these resolve through experiment and practice.

Light and Sound

The light and sound operator will be slotting the cues into the show, and that, as with everything else in this lengthy rehearsal, takes time and practice. Levels and cues for light and sound will be adjusted. The rehearsal may have to be held up for lights to be re-focused or even re-rigged. Positions may have to be marked on the stage floor if an actor has to

The designer paints some finishing touches on the set at the end of the tech.

The rehearsal stops while technicians sort out a problem with the set.

position himself precisely to be 'discovered' by a beam of light.

There may have been a sound-plotting session before the tech when cues and levels will have been set and marked. If not, the sound operator will adjust the volume levels during the tech in consultation with the director. Different cues sound from different speakers so that the sound seems to be coming from the appropriate place. The MD will not be able to judge the sound levels from his position near the stage, and relies on the sound operator and director to set the levels of mikes and sound cues.

The Costume Department

Pantomime tends to involve many costume changes. Actors are unused to wearing their costumes and though they will have imagined their changes in rehearsal and practised them in the wardrobe, the reality, once again, is a different matter. There is the added problem of working out whether quick changes can be done in the dressing room or whether they must be done at the side of the stage to save time, and whether actors can manage alone or will need help from a dresser, a member of stage management or another member of the cast. Quick changes are timed in the tech, and actor and dresser freeze if there is a hold-up, and carry on where they left off when the problem has been resolved: it is difficult for director, lighting and sound people, and so on, who are watching the rehearsal from the front of house, to remember as they sort out a troublesome cue that a desperate actor is trying a quick change for the first time. It is vital to rehearse the practicality of costume changes at this stage to allow time to put matters right before the dress rehearsal.

The Director

The pressure of getting through so much complicated technical work while keeping the actors' confidence alive and giving the technical crew the time they need for what is essentially their first rehearsal makes particular demands of the director. It is hard to control the longing to use the hour it may take to sort out a technical problem to rehearse the actors, and to remember how much the technical crew need space and time and the company's concentration to sort out problems backstage.

There are long empty silences when it appears nothing is happening onstage except perhaps a slight juddering of scenery. From the auditorium it looks as if everyone has gone off for a cup of tea. But backstage the crew are up ladders, wielding screwdrivers, and trying desperately to free the beanstalk that is refusing to rise magically from its bean. Children dressed as gnomes have become bored waiting in the wings for their entrance and are fiddling with the carefully arranged prop table, and an actor stands poised, half undressed, waiting for the problem to be solved so that he can continue timing his quick change. The pauses, while technical problems are being sorted out backstage, seem endless to anyone in the auditorium as they sit, unable to do anything but wait in the dark, and think how much rehearsal time is being gobbled up.

It is most important that everyone stays calm and retains confidence in the team. Directors and technicians may long to bury their heads in their hands and weep at the apparent chaos onstage. This does not help. When all departments work together to overcome the problem, it will resolve; with practice and a bit of reorganization the original idea will recover from its difficult birth and thrive.

Despite all the complications, it is exciting. Everyone is seeing and hearing for the first time the pictures and sounds that they have built up through rehearsals, production meetings and discussions. The edges are rough, the sounds blurred, but the spirit of the pantomime glimmers through the murk.

At last it ends; the lighting cue for the curtain call is rehearsed. The director, MD, choreographer and stage manager list anything that needs urgent rehearsal before the dress run. A schedule for the next day is produced and the actors can go home. The technicians begin work on their lists to make sure that everything is ready for the dress rehearsal.

Cooking the Technical Pudding

The most constructive way to approach a pantomime tech as director, choreographer, designer, actor or crew is to assume that nothing will be right first time, and that time and calm thought, experiment and practice will solve most problems. Time and patience are in short supply at this stage of rehearsal. Every effect is a mix of the skills of different departments and no-one in the theatre has seen all the ingredients mixed together before. The recipe has been discussed and each department has prepared its particular ingredients, but no-one has tasted the result. Time must be allowed to test the recipe and for the company to make the fine adjustments that will result in the perfect cake. The director, like the head chef, will lead the different departments of the company through this steamy preparation.

THE DRESS REHEARSAL

Pantomime dress rehearsals differ from most other theatre dress rehearsals. Pantomime relies so much on the audience reaction and participation that even the most perfect dress rehearsal is a poor foretaste, for actors, musicians and crew, of what will happen when the house is full. It is usual to add ten minutes to the rehearsed running time of the show to allow for the audience input.

The dress rehearsal, in an ideal world, should be just like the performance without the audience. Pantomime is so fast and furious, so full of possible pitfalls, that this is rarely the case. And there is an added problem. The audience has a starring role in pantomime and they are not there. The hisses and boos, the repartee and participation cannot be rehearsed, timed or scripted. Child actors usually work in teams,

Ice creams are delivered and sweet supplies are checked.

so at least the team who are not performing, and any other company members who can spare the time, can provide 'He's behind you!' for the actors onstage. The actors must imagine the audience reaction and rely on their

experience and wit to improvise to it when it is there in reality. Even at this latest stage there will be problems that have to be sorted out before the first performance.

Rehearsing the Curtain Call

The pantomime curtain call, by tradition, is a double ceremony. The first phase is the 'walk-down' when all the characters, who have been quick-changing backstage, appear in their most glamorous costumes to take their bows. The children usually appear first, followed by the dancers. Couples, such as the comedy double act or the Babes in the Wood take their bows together. The Dame, triumphant in her most outrageous hat appears second to last and the Principal Boy and Girl, happy-ever-after at last in their wedding finery, complete the line-up. They all sing their final number, often a reprise from the show, and take their final bows with an acknowledgement of the band.

FRONT OF HOUSE

Pantomime, more than any other show in a venue's calendar, draws everyone who works in the building into its company. The involvement of the audience and the presence of so many children make the whole outing a treat for the family. And the front of house staff present a vital part of this exciting occasion.

Extras Supplies

Enough sweets and ice creams must be ordered to satisfy the young customers. Another fridge may have to be hired to cope with the demand. The bar will sell many more soft drinks than usual. There may be magic wands, badges or light-sticks for sale as well as programmes. Extra front of house staff and ushers will be employed, and must be trained for their jobs.

Cleaning

Pantomimes make mess, and the front of house staff must be prepared to clear it all up so that the patrons arriving for the evening show find the theatre, both auditorium and front of house, as clean as it was for the matinee. The space between and under the seats will be awash with sweet papers and ice cream cartons. The work of the cleaners can be halved if ushers take round bin-bags as the audience are leaving and ask for their rubbish. It is against fire regulations to place litter bins in the auditorium.

Timing

The length and performance times of the shows are vital to the front of house manager. There must be time to clean and prepare between the shows. They will encourage the audience into their seats so that the curtain goes up on time and will be ready for the rush of the interval. There may be moments during the performance when they have to hold doors open or clear paths for actors whose performance involves them running round the audience or appearing from the back of the auditorium.

Beyond the Call of Front of House Duty

Several hundred excited children in the building and many of them experiencing live theatre for the first time is a heady brew. The younger ones can find it frightening and the pantomime foyer usually shields a few adults with children who are overwhelmed. Sympathetic front of house helpers can make a huge difference to the child's experience. They can explain the story, provide drinks and encourage the child to go back into the audito-

rium. They may even be responsible for turning the child from an adult who will never visit a theatre again to a regular theatre-goer who will, some future Christmas, take his own children to the pantomime and keep the ball rolling.

THE FIRST NIGHT

The first night, when the company work the show for the first time with an audience, comes as a shock to performers unless they have pantomime experience. The director has no choice but to let the actors get on with it and hope they can cope – she can do nothing to help once the curtain goes up. The musical

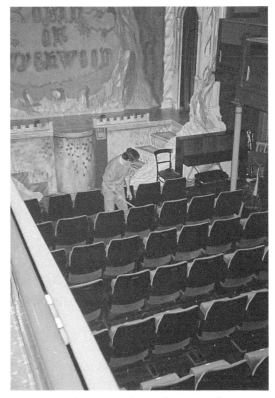

Sweeping the sweet papers between the shows.

Programme and bar proceeds boost the theatre's takings.

director, however, is there and in sight of the actors onstage – even if the audience can't see him – and can, by the way he plays and leads his band, help the performance over any hitches. His performance will remain flexible throughout the first few shows; the timing of scene changes and business speeds up during the run of the show and the music must follow suit.

First performances of pantomimes stand alone in the theatrical life of an actor. The response from the audience and the sound coming onto the stage from the children in the house cannot be imagined until you have heard it. Nothing but experience can prepare an actor for the roar of response to a 'Hullo everybody!', the laughter, and the obvious and often vocal determination that good must triumph and evil be vanquished.

An actor prepares for the first night of the pantomime.

Fashions in pantomime production come and go, but the affection and enjoyment between actor and audience as they share a familiar story remains unchanged.

BIBLIOGRAPHY

BOOKS

Bicât, T., *Making Stage Costumes – A Practical Guide* ISBN 1861264089 (Crowood, 2000)

Brewer's Theatre – A Phrase and Fable Dictionary ISBN 0304346926 (Cassell, 1994)

Fraser, N., *Stage Lighting Explained* ISBN 1861264909 (Crowood 1999)

Gardyne, J., *Staging a Musical – A Practical Guide* ISBN 1861266278 (Crowood, 2004)

Gascoigne, B., *World Theatre – An Illustrated History* ISBN 0128691804 (Ebury Press, 1968)

Gillette, A.S., *Stage Scenery: Its Construction and Rigging* (Harper & Row, 1972)

Harris, P. and Hudd, R., *The Pantomime Book – The Only Known Collection of Pantomime Jokes in Captivity* (Peter Owen, 2001)

Robbins, N., *Slapstick and Sausages* ISBN 095429871 (Trapdoor, 2002)

Tilke, M., *Costume Patterns and Designs* ISBN 084781209X (St Martin's Press, 1990)

Walne, G. (ed.) *Effects for the Theatre* ISBN 0713639857 (A. & C. Black, 1995)

Wilson, A. E., *King Panto – The Story of Pantomime* (Dutton, 1935)

Wilson, A., *Making Stage Props – A Practical Guide* ISBN 186125450X (Crowood, 2003)

Winslow, C., *The Oberon Glossary of Theatrical Terms* ISBN 1870259262 (Oberon 1991)

Wood, D. and Grant, J., *Theatre for Children* ISBN 1566632331 (Ivan R. Dee, 2000)

USEFUL WEBSITES

www.its-behind-you.com – Information, news and pictures for all pantomime enthusiasts
www.samuelfrench-london.co.uk

INDEX

INDEX